Folk Art Tells a Story

Folk Art
Tells a Story

An Activity Guide

SUSAN CONKLIN THOMPSON

Illustrations by Steve Welch

Photographs by Keith Thompson

Songs by Gretchen Young

1998
TEACHER IDEAS PRESS
A Division of
Libraries Unlimited, Inc.
Englewood, Colorado

This book is dedicated to folk artists everywhere. They inspire us, make us smile, and tell us a story with their beautiful works of art.

TEACHER IDEAS PRESS
A Division of
Libraries Unlimited, Inc.
P.O. Box 6633
Englewood, CO 80155-6633
1-800-237-6124
www.lu.com/tip

Production Editor: Kevin W. Perizzolo
Copy Editor: Jason Cook
Proofreader: Cherie Rayburn
Indexer: Nancy Fulton
Typesetter: Kay Minnis

Library of Congress Cataloging-in-Publication Data

Thompson, Susan Conklin.
    Folk art tells a story : an activity guide / Susan Conklin
Thompson ; illustrated by Steve Welch ; photographs by Keith
Thompson ; songs by Gretchen Young.
        xii, 185 p. 22x28 cm.
    Includes bibliographical references (p. 171) and index.
    ISBN 1-56308-382-5
    1. Folk art--Study and teaching (Elementary)--United States.
2. Ethnic arts--Study and teaching (Elementary)--United States.
3. Education, Elementary--Activity programs--United States.
I. Title.
NX303.T48   1998
372.5--dc21   97-33618
                                                                CIP

Contents

From the Earth

Acknowledgments

This book was an interesting and enjoyable project. I thank the people who were generous with their time and talents. Thanks to Keith Thompson, William Conklin, Beth Wilkinson, Steve Welch, Gretchen Young, Tom Smucker, Susan Rea, Ignacia Duran, Mamie Deschillie, Ronald Jean, David Gomez, Maximina Lopez, Francisca Perez DePayola, and Marsha Lorenzen. Thanks to Marcia Lorenzen for the great idea for the pattern for the clay puppets. Also thanks to my editors, Susan Zernial, Kevin W. Perizzolo, and Jason Cook, who have made this book possible, and to Suzanne Barchers, who believed I could write this book. Special thanks to my children, Kayenta and Rosalie, who are always open to new ideas. Also, thanks to children everywhere who inspire us and bring us joy with their art.

Introduction

Since I was a little girl, I have loved the simple, warm nature of folk art. Folk art tells a story of many generations of people and reflects cultures everywhere. With a little knowledge, a student examining a brightly colored Peruvian wall hanging or a carving of a shaggy Navajo goat will not only see a pleasing piece of art, but will glimpse the traditions and experiences of the people who created it. The purpose of this book is to bring the real world of folk art to students. This book is primarily an art and social studies book, but the activities also integrate language arts, music, science, and math.

Elementary-age students will enjoy learning about the folk art featured in this book, participating in the activities, and creating artwork of their own. Traditionally, folk art captures the personality and artistry of the craftsperson, and the same is true with students. Their experiences will be reflected in their artwork, and they will bring many variations and creative ideas to the activities. Each piece of artwork will be unique—a reflection of the student who created it.

Folk Art Tells a Story is divided into three sections: "Folk Art from Yesteryear" contains folk art activities that have been appreciated for many generations and that provide students with connections to and knowledge of the past. "From the Earth" involves students in activities that help them gain an appreciation for and understanding of art created by materials from the earth. "Colorful Cloth" involves students in discovering, exploring, and learning about various ways cloth is colored throughout the world.

This book contains interesting information about folk art; authentic, open-ended projects; book suggestions; songs, stories, and recipes; and oral history interviews that introduce students to actual folk artists. The integrated activities help students gain new experiences and build on previous experiences. Elementary-age students of all developmental levels will be interested in the information and activities included in this book. The students will be challenged by the open-ended nature of the activities, and the activities will be a good match for how the students learn. They will learn a lot about themselves and their classmates as they explore together and communicate their thoughts, experiences, and ideas.

Provide opportunities for the students to discuss their artwork and projects. The very nature of folk art is about sharing who you are, the culture you come from, and your experiences. Oral language is an important part of communicating with others. Take time to talk with students, and praise them for their good work and ideas.

You need not proceed sequentially from one section to the next, or from one activity to the next. Feel free to turn to any section in the book to try an interesting activity. Each activity provides information to be shared with the students, a list of materials that each student will need, step-by-step directions, and questions that will help each student explore new ideas and broaden his or her thinking. Additional ideas and activities are included with some of the activities. These ideas involve students in experiences connected to the original activity and provide children with additional information. The activities are integrated and fit in with different areas of learning, such as language arts, math, science, art, and social studies. Questions provided with the activities will expand students' thinking and guide them to new creations and inventions. Encourage the students to be creative and to explore their good ideas.

No two pieces of artwork will look just alike—they will be as varied as the students who create them. There are wonderful opportunities in this book for students to learn new things and bring their experiences and personalities into the activities. When each student sculpts an original clay puppet or mask and dyes a unique design on fabric, you will truly know that folk art tells a story.

Folk Art from Yesteryear

Grandma Moses

1—Memories

Art, Language Arts

Preparation

Show the students a print of a painting by Grandma Moses and explain that Grandma Moses's real name was Anna Mary Robertson, who lived to be 101 years old. She was a folk artist—someone who has never had formal art training. She made her first pictures by stitching yarn on canvas. When she was in her 70s, she began painting because she had developed arthritis in her hands, and it became difficult to stitch.

Grandma Moses often painted memories from her childhood. She grew up on a farm in a family of 10 children. Many of her pictures show families from everyday life. Have prints of some of her paintings available for the students to examine and discuss. Help the students study the pictures by asking them questions such as "What colors has Grandma Moses used in this scene?" and "What is happening in this scene?" *Barefoot in the Grass: The Story of Grandma Moses* (1970) by William H. Armstrong and *Grandma Moses, Painter of Rural America* (1986) by Zibby Oneal are good books to share with students.

In Laura Wilder's book *The Little House in the Big Woods* (1932), there is a passage in which Mary and Laura are playing with dolls. They talk about wanting to play "going to town" but find it difficult because they have never seen a town. Talk with the students about how we have a clearer conception of events that we have experienced and why it is often suggested that we write about or paint something we have experienced. For this reason, Grandma Moses painted the things that she experienced in her life.

Involve the students in thinking of a special memory they have and describing the memory to a friend. Have the students watch as you paint on a paper plate a memory of yours. While you paint, talk about the memory, describing it as you work.

✿ ✿ ✿

In the activity that follows, involve the students in painting their memories on paper plates.

Each Student Needs

- Paper plate (available at most grocery stores)
  To prepare the plates for the students, paint the surface of each with white household paint. (Latex paint is recommended because it dries quickly.)
- Tempera paints
- Paintbrushes
- Cups or bowls to hold paints
- Pencil
- Paper plates for mixing paints
- Sheets of paper
- Tape

Have Each Student

1. Think of a memory.
2. Optional: Sketch the memory on the plate with a pencil.
3. Paint the memory.
4. Share the painting with a classmate.
5. Write about the memory on a piece of paper and attach it to the back of the plate with a small piece of tape.

Tray

Exploring with Students

Are you painting an everyday event, such as riding the school bus, or a special occasion, such as having a family picnic? How are you choosing what to paint? Which colors are you choosing for your painting? How do these colors affect the mood of the picture?

Variation

Grandma Moses also painted on household tiles. Have the students try painting on kitchen or bathroom tiles. Ask them how this activity is like or unlike painting on paper plates.

2—Painting What You See

Science, Art, Language Arts

Preparation

People would see a scene painted by Grandma Moses and ask her to paint one just like it for them. Grandma Moses did not want to paint the same picture twice, so she observed the scene from different vantage points. She looked out one window and painted what she saw; then she looked out another window and painted the scene as viewed from the second window.

Involve the students in looking out a window and observing a scene. Have them describe what they see to another child. Have them observe the scene from another window and describe how the scene looks different.

Using watercolors, paint an outdoor scene viewed from a classroom window. Have students observe and compare the scene to what you are painting. On another piece of paper, paint the scene from another angle. Tell the students that when we observe something from different angles, we say that we are observing it "from different vantage points." Talk with the students about the differences between the paintings.

✷ ✷ ✷

In the activity that follows, involve the students in painting a scene from two different vantage points.

Each Student Needs

- Paper (Watercolor paper is preferable, but it can be expensive. Any type of white drawing or typing paper is acceptable.)
- Watercolors
- Paintbrushes
- Cups or dishes of water

Have Each Student

1. Observe a scene from various angles.
2. Paint the scene from two vantage points.

3. Share the paintings with a classmate.

Scenes from Two Perspectives

Exploring with Students

What is different about your scene when you look at it from another vantage point? How are you showing the differences in your paintings? Can you imagine what this scene might look like from a third vantage point? Do you think that sometimes people differ in their ideas because they "see" *experiences* from different vantage points? Can you give an example?

3—A New Season

Art, Science, Social Studies, Language Arts, Music

Preparation

Ask students questions about how seasons vary in length and severity from one location to another: What are the seasons like where you live? How are the seasons different where others live? Talk with the students about the current season. What is most distinctive about it?

Take the students on a nature walk to examine how the season affects the environment. What do they notice? How could they show what they see in a painting?

∅   ∅   ∅

Read the following story to the students as a prelude to painting a scene that depicts a season in their neighborhood or community.

A Colorful World

It was a warm fall day in Vermont. Ursula was going with her friend Molly and Molly's mother to a craft fair being held at a school 20 miles away. Molly's mother said that they would be driving through the country.

Ursula and Molly joked and laughed as they started out on their drive. Then Molly heard Ursula gasp in wonder.

"Look, Molly!" Ursula exclaimed.

Molly looked to see where Ursula was pointing. Out the window were some of the most beautiful trees Molly had ever seen. They were a blend of yellow, orange, and shades of red. "Wow!" said Molly. "Look at the trees."

Molly and Ursula could not take their eyes off the beautiful fall countryside. Everywhere they looked they saw patches of the brilliant colors. Before they were ready for the drive to end, they had arrived at the school.

Molly's mother asked, "What did you think of the ride through the country?"

"It was wonderful," said Molly.

"It sure was," stated Ursula. "The country looked just like a sponge painting!"

"A sponge painting!" exclaimed Molly's mother with surprise. "You know, it did at that."

Activities

1. Ask the students if they have ever made a sponge painting. What did Ursula mean when she described the fall day as looking like a sponge painting? Encourage them to describe fall days they have enjoyed, as well as winter, spring, and summer days.

2. Involve the students in singing the following song (p. 8) about the four seasons.

3. Involve the students in making a sponge painting of an outdoor scene. Provide each child with a piece of newsprint or scrap paper on which to practice and experiment before creating the scene. Older students may want to draw or paint parts of the scene using a paintbrush before and after they use the sponge. Young students may prefer sponge painting without adding these details.

COLORS OF THE SEASONS

What col- ors will you paint the year? Each sea- son has its hues; Spring,

summer, fall, and win- ter, which col- ors will you choose?

1. Fall has lots of orange and red, yel- low, brown and green;
2. Spring is fresh with shades of green, skies both gray and blue;

Win- ter is gray, brown and white, with snow so spar- kling clean.
Sum- mer glows with col- ors bright, from flow- ers and the dew.

Each Student Needs

- Newsprint or scrap paper
- White construction paper or drawing paper
- Tempera paints
- Various sizes and shapes of sponges (Damp sponges do not absorb as much paint as dry sponges and are easier to control.)
- Paintbrushes

Have Each Student

1. Think about an outdoor scene to paint.
2. Dip the flat edge of a damp sponge into the tempera paint.
3. Dab the sponge on the paper.
4. Using a paint brush, paint the details. (Steps 3 and 4 can be done in reverse order.)

Sponge Painting of a Fall Day

Exploring with Students

How is sponge painting different from painting with a brush? What words would you use to describe the texture the sponge makes with the paint?

Read to the students Ramona Maher's book *Alice Yazzie's Year* (1977), a beautiful book about the months and seasons. This book uses poetry to portray a year in the life of Alice Yazzie, a Navajo girl.

Extending Ideas

1. The story about Ursula and Molly is true. What experiences of yours with children would make good stories? Write them down and share them with students. What art projects could students do in response to your experiences and stories?

4—Folk Songs

Music, Social Studies, Emotional and Social Development, Art, Language Arts

Preparation

Grandma Moses won the New York state painting prize for her work *The Old Oaken Bucket*. It is based on a popular song she remembered singing when she was young.

The books *The Fox Went Out on a Chilly Night: An Old Song* (1961), illustrated by Peter Spier, and *When I First Came to This Land* (1965) by Oscar Brand are illustrated folk songs for children. Many of the songs have interesting histories and tell a story. Brand wrote *When I First Came to This Land* when he was asked to write a song about immigrants coming to this country.

Explain to students that folk songs, like folk stories, can be passed down in the oral tradition from generation to generation. This is why many songs and stories have variations. Ask the students to name folk songs they know. Sing some of the songs, and discuss the stories the songs tell. Discuss with students why the songs may have been written.

With the students, look at an illustrated folk song book. Talk with them about which parts of the song have been illustrated and what media were used to create the illustrations (watercolor, pencil, collage, etc.). Discuss the illustrations on the cover of the book used to represent the folk song. Ask the students why they think the book has the title it does.

✗ ✗ ✗

In the activity that follows, involve students in creating an illustrated folk song book or illustrating part of a folk song on a piece of paper.

Each Student (or Group) Needs

- Paper (white, any type)
- Color pencils, paints, paintbrushes, and other materials for illustrations
- Books containing folk songs (optional)

Have Each Student (or Group)

1. Learn a folk song.
2. Talk about folk songs in history.
3. Choose a folk song to illustrate.
4. Decide how to create the illustrations.
5. Illustrate the folk song.
6. Share the illustrated folk song with a classmate.

Folk Song Illustration

Exploring with Students

How are you deciding what to illustrate? If you are illustrating a book, are you planning where to make the page breaks? Are you illustrating the entire book using one medium, or are you combining several media?

Extending Ideas

1. Play a folk game such as the old favorite "The Farmer in the Dell." This game is a circle dance originally called "The Farmer's in His Den." The den refers to a clearing in the woods. Circle dances can be traced back to at least 1350 B.C.E. People began playing this game in America in 1883. The book *The Farmer in the Dell* (1978), with pictures by Mary Maki Rae, illustrates this game with clever folk art drawings.

2. *Emma* (1980) by Wendy Kesselman is the story of an old woman who, like Grandma Moses, paints pictures of her childhood. She, too, is a folk artist. With the students, read this story and others that contain folk art illustrations, such as *The Ox Cart* (1976) by Donald Hall, illustrated by Barbara Cooney.

3. Children are natural folk artists because most have little training. They often paint with bold lines, and their scenes are reminiscent of everyday happenings, such as swinging on a swing and hanging out clothing. Talk with the students about being folk artists, and encourage them to write a story and illustrate it with folk art.

4. The folk artist Mattie Lou O'Kelley wrote a beautiful book titled *From the Hills of Georgia* (1983). This book is an autobiography in paintings. Read the book with the students, and challenge them to create an autobiography using folk pictures to depict major events in their lives.

The Quilting Bee

1—Quilts

Social Studies, Science, Art, Language Arts

Examining a Quilt

Preparation

Ask the students about the traditions their families follow. Discuss with them how traditions are passed down from family to family, through the generations. If you have involved students in the activity "Memories" (p. 3), have them talk about any scenes they painted that show family traditions, such as a holiday meal or family vacation. Encourage the students to ask their families about traditions that have been passed down to them. Have students discuss which traditions they would like to pass down to their children.

Quilts were an important part of the households of many people's ancestors. The houses did not have many rooms, and the quilts decorated the rooms in a personal way. Quilts played a role in social gatherings. Quilting bees were quite common. At a quilting bee, people would gather together and create a quilt from cloth that was no longer needed for anything else. Many people's ancestors were definitely recyclers! Ask students if they have ever recognized pieces of their leftover clothing in a family quilt.

Traditional quilting square patterns include:

Show students examples of quilts, or have illustrations available for them to examine.

✄ ✄ ✄

In the activity that follows, involve students in making a quilt from wallpaper samples. Have the students try a traditional pattern, or encourage them to design an original pattern or picture.

Each Student Needs

- Wallpaper sample books (available at local paint and wallpaper stores)
- Glue
- Scissors
- Pencil
- Construction paper

Have Each Student

1. Design a quilt square on paper.
2. Cut wallpaper samples into pieces needed to create quilt square.
3. Glue the pieces onto a sheet of paper.
4. Tell about the square.
5. As a class, combine squares together to make a group quilt. Use a large piece of butcher paper and tape the individual squares side by side. (Put tape on back of squares.)

Paper Quilt Square

Exploring with Students

Are you planning a pattern or a picture for your square? Why are you selecting these particular wallpaper samples? Are you coordinating colors?

Extending Ideas

1. Tomi dePaola's book *The Quilt Story* (1985) and Valerie Flournoy's book *The Patchwork Quilt* (1985) tell lovely stories about quilts. Read these books to the students and talk about the stories. Reading works of historical fiction is one way to help students understand and appreciate how history relates to their lives.

2. Discuss quilts as a statement or memorial: The AIDS quilt is a quilt that represents many people who have died of AIDS. Each square on the quilt represents a person and is designed in a unique manner. The quilt covers more than 32 acres when unfolded. The quilt panels were made by friends, family members, and others who cared about the person with AIDS. Quilt panels are displayed in various locations all over the world. Many different materials are used in a panel. These include such things as records, pearls, photographs, stuffed animals, and wedding rings. Each square or panel reflects the personality of the person it represents.

3. Simple quilts can be made by combining fabric and paper. Have each student draw a picture or design a quilt square on a piece of paper. Tape or staple the squares onto a large piece of fabric, leaving space between each picture to create a fabric border around each square. Another method is to have each student illustrate or design a muslin square using fabric crayons or markers. Stitch the squares together to create an interesting wall hanging. The quilt might have a theme, such as the state's history, pets, or families.

4. Some people cut old quilts into pieces to make pillows, stuffed toys, or even Christmas stockings. Talk with the students about recycling and explain that quilts were originally made from scraps of fabric saved from favorite dresses, shirts, and other clothing. Today, when people cut a worn quilt into pieces to make something else, they are recycling in the same way their ancestors did when they made the original quilts. Have the students discuss other ways we recycle materials today.

5. Involve students in singing the following song, "Quilts."

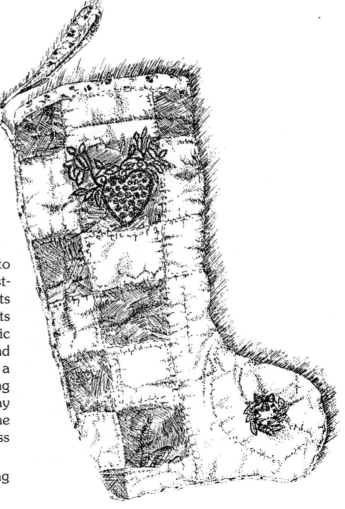

Quilted Stocking

QUILTS

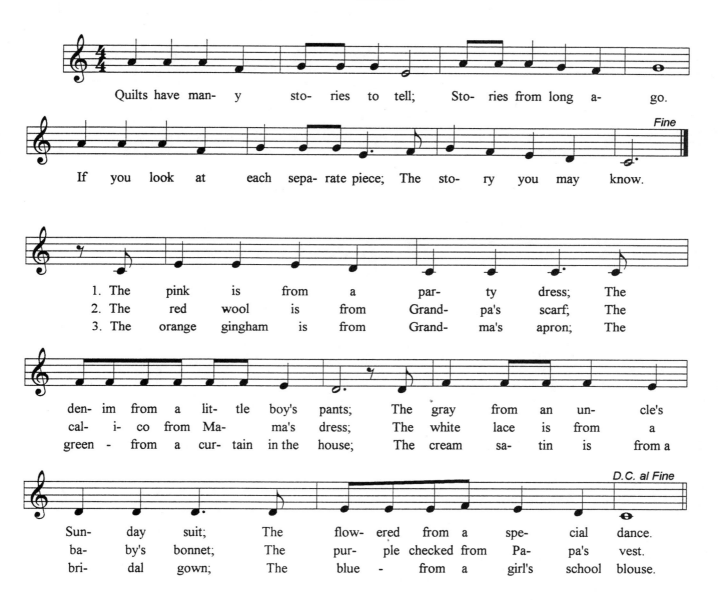

Quilts have man- y sto- ries to tell; Sto- ries from long a- go.

Fine

If you look at each sepa- rate piece; The sto- ry you may know.

1. The pink is from a par- ty dress; The
2. The red wool is from Grand- pa's scarf; The
3. The orange gingham is from Grand- ma's apron; The

den- im from a lit- tle boy's pants; The gray from an un- cle's
cal- i- co from Ma- ma's dress; The white lace is from a
green - from a cur- tain in the house; The cream sa- tin is from a

D.C. al Fine

Sun- day suit; The flow- ered from a spe- cial dance.
ba- by's bonnet; The pur- ple checked from Pa- pa's vest.
bri- dal gown; The blue - from a girl's school blouse.

6. Read to students *My Grandmother's Patchwork Quilt: A Book and Pocketful of Patchwork Pieces* (1993/94) by Sheri Safran, which contains actual fabric quilt squares that can be pieced together to accompany the story. The students will enjoy completing the patterned squares and sewing them together to make a quilt.

7. Quilts are just one historical craft or art. Involve students in researching an historical craft of interest, such as shoeing horses, or making syrup, butter, or candles. Encourage the students to learn all they can about their topic. This might include conducting an oral history interview with someone who has shod horses, about the process and its history; or experimenting to make butter with a jar or churn.

    Involve the students in comparing today's time period with the time period when the craft was at its peak. For example, if the students are investigating making dipped candles, they might compare how often electricity is used during a typical modern day to how often candles were used during a typical day before the invention of electricity. Have students discuss how different their day would be if there were no electricity and all artificial light came from a candle.

    Help students research the craft to its origin and compare its forms and functions historically. For example, various types of candles have been used for light, but today, candles are typically used for religious purposes and other special occasions. Discuss with students how they use candles in their homes and how they have seen candles used in other settings.

8. Read a book to the students that contains illustrations of pioneer life in the woods or on the prairie. Talk about how the lifestyle influenced the crafts. Have each child keep a sketchbook as a visual journal to record some of their experiences. On a regular basis, have students sketch a scene or event from their life. Have students use their sketchbooks as a source of ideas for creative writing activities.

2—Faith Ringgold

Social Studies, Art, Language Arts

Preparation

Faith Ringgold is an African American artist who is well known for her elaborate story quilts and her beautiful children's books. Robyn Montana Turner's book *Faith Ringgold: Portraits of Women Artists for Children* (1993) tells about Faith's life as a young girl in Harlem, her development into a strong young woman, and the wonderful artwork she created along the way. As an adult artist, Faith is famous for painting a scene on canvas, sewing on the canvas a border in which she writes (paints) about the scene, and then completing the work with a quilted border around the edge.

Like Grandma Moses (see p. 3), Faith often paints about her experiences. For example, her popular quilt *Tar Beach* shows a family playing cards at a table on the roof of an apartment building while two girls are spread out on an old mattress on the tar-paper roof. Faith also wrote a children's book about these memories, *Faith Ringgold: Tar Beach* (1991).

∅ ∅ ∅

In the activity that follows, involve students in creating a story quilt of their own. Encourage them to brainstorm memories they would like to communicate to other people through art. Talk with them about how a picture portrays ideas and emotions. Have students write a message to add to their quilt that will highlight the picture they have painted. They may want to highlight the picture by writing a poem, a description of the event, or thoughts that continue the ideas and emotions portrayed in the painting.

Each Student Needs

- Large sheet of white construction paper
- Tempera or acrylic paints
- Paintbrushes
- Quilt materials (wallpaper samples, wrapping paper, scraps of fabric, etc.)
- Scissors
- Glue
- Black ink pen or thin black marker
- 8-by-8-inch square of muslin canvas (optional)

Have Each Student

1. Think of a memory (or an ensemble of memories) to paint and write about for an audience.
2. Paint a scene from the memory on a piece of white construction paper (or muslin). Leave a white border around the picture if on paper. On muslin there is no need for a border.
3. If using muslin, staple it onto a large piece of white construction paper. (Staple each corner of the muslin after centering the muslin square on the paper.)
4. Cut small and large squares from the wallpaper, wrapping paper, and fabric (a combination of these materials or only one type).
5. Glue the small squares along the top and bottom edges of the muslin, or around the scene if it has been painted on paper. (Glue the squares on the back side so a white border remains.)
6. Glue the large squares around the outer edge of the picture.
7. Using a black ink pen or a thin black marker, write a poem, thoughts, or a description of the scene around the border.
8. Share the story quilt with a classmate.

Exploring with Students

Are you painting a representation of one experience or of several experiences? Does your writing highlight what you have painted?

Extending Activities

1. Share with students *Aunt Harriet's Underground Railroad in the Sky* (1992) by Faith Ringgold.

Story Quilt

Clues from the Past

1—Colored Bottles

Art, Social Studies, Language Arts, Science

Preparation

Colored Bottles

Colored bottles sparkle in the grass, halfway hidden in the dirt around deserted houses in many old mining towns. Colored bottles and pieces of glass are authentic artifacts of the people who struggled daily to make their living from the minerals that come from the earth. Some bottles originally were colored and sat on counters or tables in small kitchens. Other bottles gradually changed color—to light blue, purple, and rose—as the sun shone upon them.

✇ ✇ ✇

Read the story below to the students as a prelude to the activities that follow.

Questions in a Box

Collection day at school was an exciting time for Annie and her friends. Ever since Mrs. Schaack, their third-grade teacher, asked them to bring their collections to school on Thursday, they had been excitedly discussing what they would bring.

On Thursday, Annie's friends got out their interesting collections. Josie had her stuffed bear collection. She had been collecting bears since she was born. Josie had bears of all sizes and colors, even one wearing a nurse's outfit that her grandma had given her when her tonsils became infected and she had to go to the hospital to have them taken out. Michelle had so many bead necklaces that Annie thought surely it must have taken a wheelbarrow to bring them all to school. It got a little boring hearing where all the necklaces came from, and what seemed like a million other stories to go with that many necklaces. Tony had a fun collection of marbles, and he showed how to shoot with a cat's eye. It made a loud smack when it hit the marbles. Marbles went everywhere, and Mrs. Schaack had him go around the classroom right then and pick them up.

When it was Annie's turn to show her collection, she got out an old shoe box. In the box were many pieces of colored glass. Some pieces were light rose, others lilac, and some turquoise blue. Annie told how she and her family had gone to old mining towns and looked on the hillsides for broken glass. Then she held a pretty piece of rose glass up to the light, and, as the sun shone through the glass, all her friends talked about how pretty it looked (all except Josie, of course, who didn't want anyone to have something neater than her bears).

The children had lots of questions when Annie told them that the glass originally was clear, but the sun shining on the pieces had slowly changed their color. The children were interested in how the sun could do this. Mrs. Schaack also told them that many people make things with colored glass and then hang the "stained glass" in their windows so the sun can shine through it.

Tony had a good question. He asked Annie, "What can you tell about the people who lived there by looking at the glass?"

"I'm still thinking about that," said Annie.

Mrs. Schaack smiled. "Maybe what we have here is a box of *questions*," she said. "We can go to the library and look for a book about mining towns, and maybe another about antique bottles, to answer these questions."

After Annie had finished showing her collection, she placed the box of broken glass on the window sill. Mrs. Schaack took out a piece of glass and showed the children how to hold the glass carefully so they would not cut themselves. During free time that day, children went to the window and held up pieces of glass to see how pretty they looked in the sunlight. Annie helped her classmates examine the glass.

Activities

1. Have the students bring to class a variety of clear bottles without labels. Fill the bottles three-quarters full with water. Color the water in each bottle with food coloring. Arrange the bottles on a table or counter where sunlight will shine through them.

2. Bring to class pieces of colored glass or stained glass for the students to examine in the sunlight. (Use only glass with dull edges, and show students how to handle the glass safely.)

3. Ask the students (and people in the community) to bring artifacts to class. Have each student share their artifact and tell a story about the people who used it. Students should feel free to embellish as they wish.

4. Hold a collection day. Have each child bring to school a collection to share with the class.

Preserving a Piece of Nature

1—Pressed Flowers

Science, Art, Language Arts

Preparation

Read Tomi dePaola's book *The Legend of the Indian Paintbrush* (1988) to the students and show them photographs of different wildflowers. Ask students if they can name the state flower. Can they name state flowers for other states? Can they identify local flowers by sight? If possible, take the students on a nature walk to identify flowers. Simple guidebooks detailing many varieties of flowers can be purchased at most bookstores or borrowed from most libraries. The students will enjoy locating the flowers and pronouncing and learning their names.

Traditionally, people have admired and pressed a variety of flowers, at times using them for decorative purposes.

🌿 🌿 🌿

In the activity that follows, involve students in pressing flowers and mounting them in a scrapbook or using them to decorate bookmarks and other personal items.

Each Student Needs
- Flower guidebooks
- Flowers
- Two pieces of cardboard, slightly larger than the largest flower to be pressed
- Two pieces of felt (same size as the cardboard)
- Several thick, heavy books (phonebooks, catalogs, etc.)
- White tagboard, clear contact paper, paper punch, yarn, scissors (optional)

Have Each Student
1. Use a guidebook to identify the flowers.
2. Choose a flower and place it carefully between two pieces of felt.
3. Place the felt-enveloped flower between pieces of cardboard.

4. Place a heavy book on top of the cardboard.

5. After about four days, check the flower to see whether or not it has dried.

6. Optional: To mount dried flowers: Carefully lay the flower on a piece of white tagboard. Lay contact paper over the flower and the entire sheet of tagboard. Trim the contact paper as needed after mounting the flower.

    To make a simple bookmark: Cut a piece of thin white tagboard into a bookmark shape, lay a flower on the tagboard, and cover the front and back of the bookmark with contact paper. Make sure the contact paper extends beyond the tagboard about 1 inch at the top and ⅛ inch around the other edges. Punch a hole at the top of the bookmark and tie on a piece of yarn to make a tassel.

Exploring with Students

Can you identify the flowers you are pressing? Can you describe each flower's texture, color, and shape?

Extending Ideas

1. Students will also enjoy identifying and pressing leaves. *Look What I Did with a Leaf!* (1993) by Morteza Sohi is a lovely book that depicts common animals and natural scenes created with leaves.

Bookmark with Pressed Flower

Cookie Jars

1—Creating a Cookie Jar

Art, Social Studies, Science, Math

Preparation

To many people, cookie jars represent warmth, children, caring adults, and generations of warm family gatherings. These associations are one reason why cookie jars are popular folk art for many collectors and for many families who want a colorful, unusual addition for their kitchen.

Ask each student to bring a cookie jar to class. Have several of your own on hand for students who may not have cookie jars. Place the cookie jars on a table. With the students, examine the designs, shapes, colors, glazes, and sizes. Explain that there are many cookie jars around the nation and that many people collect cookie jars. Some people have entire rooms in their houses devoted to unusual cookie jars!

Ask the students what kind of cookie jar they would design if they were in charge of a company that made cookie jars.

🍪 🍪 🍪

In the activity that follows, involve students in creating original cookie jar designs.

Each Student Needs
- Any white drawing or typing paper
- Pencil
- Markers, paints, and paintbrushes

Have Each Student
1. Draw a picture of a cookie jar on a sheet of paper. (Encourage students to use as much white space as they can.)
2. Paint and color the cookie jar drawing.
3. Share the cookie jar design with a classmate.

Cookie Jar Drawing by a Child

Exploring with Students

Is your design well suited for filling with cookies? Can a hand fit into your jar?

Extending Ideas

1. Ask students which cookie jar (of those brought to class) can hold the most cookies. Graph their answers on a simple bar graph, with the names of jar designs along one axis and number of cookies along the other axis. Have a bag of unshelled peanuts available. Have students pretend that the peanuts are cookies, and ask them how many peanuts each jar can hold. Have each student estimate the amount each jar will hold. Write their estimates on index cards, and tape the cards to the jars. Involve the students in filling each of the jars and recording how many peanuts each jar holds. Write the totals on the card below the estimates.

2. If kitchen facilities are available, have students shell the peanuts (from the activity above) to make peanut butter (recipe below), and then use the peanut butter to make cookies (recipe on p. 28). Put the cookies into a classroom cookie jar.

Peanut Butter
Makes one cup

2½ cups shelled peanuts
2 tablespoons softened margarine
¾ teaspoon salt (or to taste)

1. Put the peanuts in a blender or food processor, about ½ cup at a time. Blend until the peanuts are chopped into small pieces.
2. Add the margarine and blend for 15 seconds at a time, stopping to scrape the sides of the blender with a spoon. Blend to desired consistency.
3. Refrigerate the peanut butter for 1 hour.

Have available store-bought peanut butter for a class "taste test." Have students compare homemade peanut butter to store-bought peanut butter. Spread the remaining peanut butter onto celery, eat it plain, and use it to make cookies.

Peanut Butter Cookies

Favorite Peanut Butter Cookies
Makes three dozen

½ cup peanut butter
¼ cup shortening
½ cup granulated sugar
½ cup packed brown sugar
¼ cup margarine (softened)

1 egg
¾ teaspoon baking soda
1¼ cups all-purpose flour
½ teaspoon baking powder

1. Mix together the peanut butter, margarine, egg, and sugars.
2. Add the remaining ingredients.
3. Chill for 4 hours.
4. Roll dough into 1" balls. Mash balls with a fork. Bake at 375° F on an ungreased cookie sheet for 9–10 minutes.

Peanut Butter Cookies

3. Play the following chant game with students. One student begins by pointing at another student and saying their name (Susan in this example):

"Susan stole the cookie from the cookie jar."
Susan responds, "Who me?"
The class responds, "Yes, you!"
Susan responds, "Couldn't be!"
The class responds, "Then who?"
Susan points at another student and begins the chant again.

Houses and Folk Art

1—Charlie Fields

Social Studies, Art, Language Arts

Preparation

Folk art is many things to different people. Some people view folk art as "childlike," while others view it as art that is highly aesthetic, created with homely tools and materials. There are people who think that true folk art must be always original and never repeated. There are people who think that any work of art that represents the common folk can be classified as folk art. Today, many types of art are considered folk art.

Acquaint students with the life and work of folk artist Charlie Fields. Charlie Fields lived in the country by a creek. When he was in his middle to late 40s, he began painting polka-dot designs on virtually everything he owned. The outside of his house was covered with polka dots and line patterns of various colors. The inside, even the furniture, was decorated with dots. He even built bee hives that looked like his house and covered them with polka dots.

Charlie Fields's House

29

Charlie had an outfit of clothing decorated with polka dots, and he would put on this outfit when he had visitors. The book *Contemporary American Folk Artists* (1975) by Elinor Horwitz contains fascinating photographs of Charlie Fields's art.

∅ ∅ ∅

In the activity that follows, involve students in creating a house from a sheet of cardboard. Lead the students in decorating their houses with folk art designs. Encourage them to be creative. A fun book to share with students is *The Big Orange Spot* (1977) by Daniel Manus Pinkwater, which emphasizes creative approaches to decorating homes.

Each Student Needs

- Pieces of cardboard or white tagboard
- Colored construction paper
- Glue
- Scissors
- Pencil
- Tempera paints
- Paintbrushes
- Markers

Have Each Student

1. Draw the outline of a house on a piece of cardboard or tagboard.
2. Cut out the house.
3. Decorate the house using paint, markers, and construction paper.
4. Share the house with a classmate.

Exploring with Students

Why did you build the house that you did? How would you heat your home? For what climate is your home best suited? What plants would you use to landscape the area around your house? Where could you live to ensure that these plants thrive?

Variation

Have students decorate a shoe, flowerpot, basket, or other ordinary household object in a fun way. Flowerpots and baskets might be painted with flowers and other designs. An undercoat of paint on the pot or basket smoothes the surface and provides a plain background. A child I know purchased a large, old lamp from the Salvation Army. She painted backgrounds for fall, winter, spring, and summer. She attached white fabric to represent snow in the winter scene; made leaf prints in the fall panel scene; added twine to an ocean setting to complete the summer scene; and designed a three-dimensional pussy willow, wrapping upward on the shade, for the spring scene.

Painted Basket

2—A Home for You

Social Studies, Language Arts, Art,
Emotional and Social Development, Music

Preparation

All around the world, people live in different types of housing. Ask students to name as many types of dwellings as they can. A beautiful book to read with the students is *Houses and Homes* (1992) by Ann Morris. This book contains wonderful photographs of various homes, as does Bobbie Kalman's book *Homes Around the World* (1994). Discuss with students types of homes, such as apartments, trailer houses, townhouses, huts, treehouses, hogans, and houseboats. Other people live temporarily in shelters and in cars. Discuss the practicality of different dwellings and reasons people may be inhabiting them. Guide students in thinking about how climate, finances, availability, and need influence where and how children and their families live.

∅ ∅ ∅

In the activity that follows, involve students in making a mural of various types of dwellings.

Each Group Needs

- Long sheet of butcher paper
- Paints, paintbrushes, markers, fabrics, and miscellaneous art supplies
- Glue
- Scissors

Have Each Group

1. Choose a community to depict, and decide where in the world the community might be. Think about how the climate, the industry, food and water sources, and so on affect the community.
2. Plan appropriate dwellings to include in a mural (see p. 32).
3. Using paints, markers, fabric, and other art supplies, create a mural.
4. Write an explanation of how the dwellings satisfy the needs of the people in the area they have selected. For example, if students have chosen to depict a community by the sea—with apartment buildings and houseboats—they might explain that many people would live in the apartments and houseboats.

Exploring with Students

How does the climate influence the types of dwellings that are built in this community? For example, if the community is a city or town by the water, are the dwellings different from dwellings in a desert community?

Various Dwellings

Extending Ideas

1. Divide the class into groups, and have each group create a mural depicting a community in a different part of the world. For example, one group might create a village in Africa and another an adobe community in the southwestern United States or the Middle East. For an interesting alternative to creating a mural, have students create model dwellings using boxes, refrigerator crates, and other building materials, such as wood or straw bales.

2. Talk with the students about how a rural area grows into an urban area. Guide them in brainstorming the differences between these areas. Students might mention that an urban area has a greater variety of houses, more businesses, and often more violence. Discuss with students the advantages and disadvantages of living in urban and rural communities. Talk with them about how a small community grows into a city. A good book that depicts this growth is *What Is a Community?* (1967) by Edward Radlauer and Ruth Shaw Radlauer.

    Divide the class into two groups. Have one group create a mural depicting a rural community and the other group a mural depicting an urban area. Display the murals of the communities on a classroom wall labeled "A Rural Community Grows into an Urban Area" or "A Small Town Grows into a City."

Community Growth

3. Discuss the information included in the above section about rural communities that grow into urban areas. On a sheet of paper, have each student draw a rural community. Help the students tape a clear overlay on top of their drawing. (An overlay from an overhead transparency works well.) Tape the overlay along the top of the drawing. Have students use markers to add to the overlay new buildings, roads, signs, and other objects that are characteristic of a city or large town. Students can hold up the overlay to see a small town, then lay down the overlay to see the town grow into a larger community.

Overlay Showing Community Growth

4. Talk with the students about what makes a house a home. Involve them in singing the following song about various dwellings that people inhabit.

PEOPLE LIVE IN DIFFERENT DWELLINGS

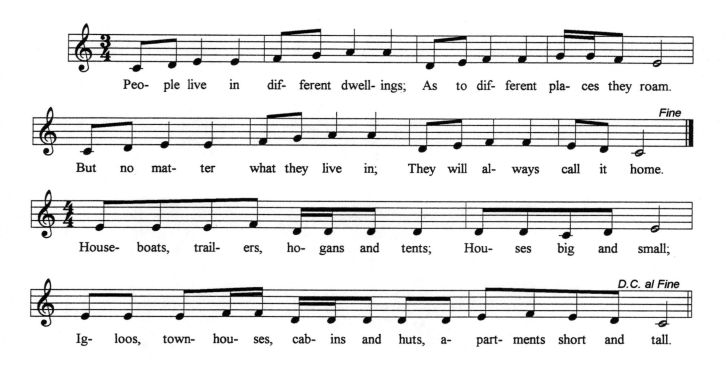

Peo- ple live in dif- ferent dwell- ings; As to dif- ferent pla- ces they roam.

But no mat- ter what they live in; They will al- ways call it home.

House- boats, trail- ers, ho- gans and tents; Hou- ses big and small;

Ig- loos, town- hou- ses, cab- ins and huts, a- part- ments short and tall.

3—Mi Casa (My House)

Art, Social Studies, Language Arts

Preparation

Houses made from stones, mud, and stones and mud are traditional to New Mexico and other areas of the Southwest. Native Americans or Ancestral Puebloans inhabited the Four Corners region of the United States (Utah, Arizona, Colorado, and New Mexico) for more than 2,000 years. They left the area, for a still-unknown reason, about 1200 C.E. Some of these peoples were cliff dwellers, who built their stone-and-mud homes in large caves near the top of deep canyons. Mesa Verde National Park encompasses several of these dwellings.

Mesa Verde Ruin

The students will enjoy hearing the following story about a field trip to an Ancestral Puebloan ruin.

Walls of Mud and Stone

The sun shone hotly, causing small beads of sweat to break out onto Kallie's neck. The forest ranger was talking about how the Ancestral Native Americans had lived in the pueblo at the base of the canyon more than 800 years ago.

The ranger concluded his introductory talk, and the group, of which Kallie was a part, were ready to begin the tour. The ranger had made sure that everyone was in good shape before they began the hike. He had asked questions about health problems and had told the group what to expect. Kallie pulled down her baseball cap tightly onto her head, keeping the autumn sun from her eyes as she began the hike. She kept one eye on her mom, to stay within sight, as they began walking down the twisting trail into the canyon.

It was a long walk to the base of the canyon. It was fun to hike on the dusty trail through the oak leaves, which were just beginning to change color. A man called out, "A tarantula!" The group rushed over to see the spider. Kallie squirmed under the man's arm and saw a large, fuzzy spider slowly crossing the trail. It stood up on its hind legs and waved its front legs, trying to scare away the people. Kallie was fascinated, and then a little disappointed when the spider finally walked into the brush on the other side of the trail.

At the base of the canyon was a little stream flowing peacefully along. The ranger showed the group how to cross a log that lay across the stream. On the other side of the stream was the Ancestral Puebloan ruin, under the overhang of a red, rock cliff. The ranger told them that the Ancestral Puebloans made their houses out of rocks and mud. The houses were very well built, and parts still remain today! He pointed out the logs that had been used for the beams of the house and the windows and doorways.

In the ruin were several medium-sized rooms—the houses—and one very large circular room. "This is the kiva," said the ranger. "It was used for ceremonies." All the people on the tour walked around inside the kiva, trying to imagine what it would have been like to have lived and performed ceremonies in these buildings so long ago. They were careful not to touch anything or pick up anything that lay around or in the ruins.

It was a hard walk back up the canyon because the trail was steep and the sun was hot. When they got back to the visitor's center, everyone drank cool water from a drinking fountain. Kallie drank water for a long time, so long in fact that the ranger asked her to please finish so there would be water left for someone else. Kallie thought of the people who had lived in the pueblo so long ago. "They must have been thirsty a lot," she thought, "living at the bottom of that hot canyon. I bet they drank the water from the stream and maybe even went swimming on hot days like today." Suddenly, Kallie wished she could experience the life of these people more than 800 years ago.

Read to students Stephen Trimble's book *The Village of Blue Stone* (1990), which describes life in an Ancestral Puebloan pueblo.

Today's Pueblo Native Americans of New Mexico and Arizona are thought to be descendants of the Ancestral Puebloan. The Ancestral Puebloan built their homes with mud-mortared sandstone bricks. Some Pueblo Native Americans live in adobe houses, with bricks made of soil mixed with clay.

Adobe bricks are made by mixing together sandy soil and clay. This mixture is poured or shoveled into wood molds and dried in the sun. A house made from adobe bricks is warm in the winter and cool in the summer. Because adobe houses are popular and charming, small models are made for doll houses, refrigerator magnets, candle holders, and even Christmas tree ornaments—folk art representing the warmth of these earth homes.

Read to students MaryLou M. Smith's book *Grandmother's Adobe Dollhouse* (1984; the English version of *La abuelita y su casa de munecas* [1993]), which tells about an adobe dollhouse and its furnishings, including some history about traditional adobe houses. Show students photographs of adobe houses, and discuss the characteristic features of adobe houses, such as covered porches and floor tiles.

❧ ❧ ❧

In the activity that follows, have students make a model adobe house using clay bricks, complete with features characteristic of adobe homes.

Each Student Needs

- Clay
- Piece of heavy cardboard
- Plastic knife
- Red or brown construction paper or thin cardboard for roof
- Optional: Tempera paint and paintbrush, small pieces of wood (such as Popsicle sticks) for doors, shutters, porch railings, roof beams, and gates

Have Each Student

1. Roll out a long, thin coil of clay (about ⅜ to ½ inch in diameter). Flatten the coil to a thickness of about ¼ inch. Turn the coil and flatten to a width of about ⅜ inch.
2. Cut the coil to make small bricks.
3. Place bricks on the cardboard in a single layer, arranging them in the shape of a house.
4. Add rows of bricks to build the walls. Build windows and doorways into the walls, or cut them out of the walls after the house has been built.
5. Add a roof by laying a piece of red or brown construction paper or painted cardboard on top of the walls.
6. Add details to the house, such as small pieces of wood for doors and shutters, wood sticks for porch railings, and strips of wood for roof beams. Build an adobe wall and a gate around the house if desired. Make a string of dried peppers from construction paper or cornhusks to hang from the roof of the porch (see ristras on pp. 97–98).

Adobe House

Exploring with Students

What problems, if any, are you having as you create your model adobe house? How can you solve these problem? What details might you add to your house to add to its old adobe charm?

Photograph of Brick Making in Williamsburg

Many of the colonial-day houses in the United States were made from adobe bricks. In the photograph above, a girl is pressing a mud mixture into a wood mold to make a brick. The bricks were dried on the ground in the sun and then used to make buildings in the famous re-created colonial village in Williamsburg, Virginia.

4—Sod Houses

Social Studies, Language Arts, Art

Sod House

Preparation

What is a sod house? Similar to adobe bricks (which are made from a mixture of sandy soil and clay), sod blocks are cut from the grassy hills—the grass roots soil holds the blocks together. Many pioneers made houses from sod because it was readily available. Some students may have seen illustrations of sod houses in which grass and flowers are shown growing on the roof! Discuss sod houses with the students, and show them the illustration (above) and other drawings and photographs. Explain that the texture of a sod house is rough because of the dirt wall.

✇ ✇ ✇

In the activity that follows, involve the students in replicating a sod house from a block of wood.

Each Student Needs

- Small block of wood: 4 inches long by 3½ inches wide by 2½ inches high (or any other dimensions that allow the block to resemble a house)
    From one 4-by-3½-inch side, use a wood chisle and eye protector to cut a triangular wedge, ½ inch deep (cut into the 4-by-2½-inch side), to make a sloped roof. Or leave the block flat on top, to depict a sod house with a flat roof (see illustration, p. 42). Warn students about sharp tools.
- Tempera paints (light yellow or beige, brown, green, and colors for flowers)
- Sawdust
- Paintbrushes

- Dried moss for roof (available at most craft stores)
- Glue

Have Each Student

1. Mix sawdust into the light yellow or beige paint.
2. Paint the house using the paint-sawdust mixture.
3. When the paint-sawdust layer is dry, paint on a roof, doors, windows, and other features, such as flower boxes.
4. When the paint is dry, glue the dry moss onto the roof.
5. Write about the differences between the sod house and the house the student inhabits. Have each student share their house and writing with a classmate.

Block-of-Wood Sod House

Exploring with Students

Why do we not live in sod houses today? Could an apartment building be made from sod?

Extending Ideas

1. Have students research sod house construction, especially roofs, windows, and doors.
2. Purchase a small amount of sod from a local lawn and garden shop. Have students trim the grass on top of the sod as short as possible and cut the sod into small blocks. Have each student construct a model sod house. They may need to "stalk" the walls with small nails to hold the sod blocks together. The sod blocks should overlap like the bricks of a modern building (this is particularly important at the corners of the house). Have students add a roof and windows using sticks, construction paper, and so on.

   Have students cut various shapes of blocks and create different types of homes, such as a townhouse, an apartment building, and a trailer home. (For other house ideas and discussion topics, see pp. 31–34.)

5—Hogans

Social Studies, Language Arts, Art

Preparation

Hogans have been homes to the Navajo people for many years. A hogan is a six-sided house made from wood and mud.

Read to students Margaret Kahn Garaway's book *The Old Hogan* (1991), which tells the story of a personified hogan who is heartbroken because the family is building a newer, more modern home. The author explains how the hogan is not only a house but also a place where the earth mother can nurture a family as they grow, laugh, face everyday problems together, and hold ceremonies to celebrate life. In this story, the little hogan sighs with relief when she discovers that she still is valuable and has a special place in the family. Her family comes to her for a very special occasion—a granddaughter's marriage.

Traditionally, many hogans were made by thickly packing mud around a cedar log frame to create one large room. The roof, too, was made by packing mud on cedar logs, which kept the hogan warm in the winter and cool in the summer. Hogans had, and still have earth floors packed hard from use, and often a stove (or fire pit in older ones) at the center of the room for cooking and heating. The hogans served the Navajo well for many years, and, although many Navajo have built houses with more rooms, running water, and electricity, some still have their old hogan on their property to use for ceremonies.

Hogan

The photograph (*see* p. 43) shows a hogan on the Navajo reservation. It is one of the older hogans on the reservation, built by packing mud around a six- or eight-sided cedar log frame and on a domed, cedar log roof made with log courses laid successively closer to the center (corbelled). Tell the students that in a playground on the reservation, small hogan playhouses have been built for the children.

Like small replicas of other types of houses, models of hogans are charming works of folk art.

∅ ∅ ∅

In the activity that follows, challenge the students to replicate a traditional hogan using sticks and clay.

Each Student Needs

- Small, flat board or piece of cardboard for a base
- Sticks (thin branches or twigs that can be cut or broken easily)
- A coping saw or hacksaw, used by an adult or under adult supervision
- Wood glue (available at hardware and discount stores)
- Potter's clay (available at most ceramic stores)
- Optional: Popsicle sticks or cardboard for doors and windows, model goats, model garden vegetables such as corn and pumpkins, dirt and plants to place around the hogan

Hogan

Have Each Student

1. Measure and break or cut the sticks 4–5 inches in length.
2. Build the walls of the model hogan by gluing the sticks together.
3. Lay sticks across the top of the hogan to make a roof. A flat roof is acceptable at this point.
4. Pack clay around the sides and on the top of the hogan (see photograph, p. 43) to make the dome.
5. Press sticks into the clay to create doors and window frames. Popsicle sticks would also work well. For a more simplistic approach, cardboard cut into door and window shapes can be pressed onto the clay as it is drying.
6. Add goats, a garden, and other accessories around the hogan to complete the model.

Exploring with Students

What are some advantages of living in a six- or eight-sided, domelike house? Where do you hold family ceremonies?

Birdhouses

1—Build a Birdhouse

Science, Social Studies, Language Arts, Art

Birdhouses

Preparation

Birdhouses are made in many styles and decorated in a variety of ways. What kinds of birdhouses have the students seen? How were they decorated?

✷ ✷ ✷

In the activity that follows, involve the students in designing and creating birdhouses. Caution the students about the entrances in the birdhouses—they should be large enough for a bird but small enough that the bird's enemies will not be able to enter. Help the students identify the birds in their area (a bird guidebook works well) so they can determine how large the entrance should be for the birds that may use the birdhouse.

Use of precut wood with holes drilled (if needed) is advised for younger students. Older students may enjoy cutting and drilling their own wood. This should be done under adult supervision only and after students have been made aware of safety precautions they must take.

Traditional Birdhouse

- Wood (1 x 6-inch pine)
- Nails (4 penny)
- Small hammer
- Paint (use an exterior, latex enamel paint)
- Paintbrushes
- Dowel
- Wood glue (available at hardware and discount stores)

Students will probably be most familiar with this traditional style of birdhouse, which can be any size. Following the illustration, cut out the sides, roof, and base of the house. Nail together the house. Using outdoor house paint, decorate the house. Add wood trim if desired (to make a Victorian-style birdhouse). Use a short section of a dowel for a perch: Drill a hole the size of the dowel below the entrance, place a few drops of glue into the hole, and insert the dowel.

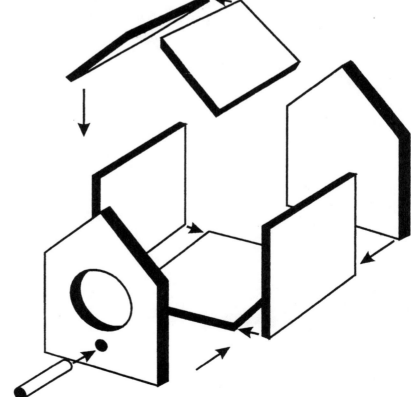

Traditional Birdhouse

Variations of the Traditional Birdhouse

1. Make a "log" birdhouse by stacking thin branches around the edges of a square wood base. Trim, notch (for overlap at corners), and sand the branches first so they can be stacked easily. Use nails (2 penny) and glue to hold the walls together. (Or, build a traditional birdhouse, and glue or nail the branches to the sides and top of the birdhouse.) Drill or saw out the entrance.

2. Make an A-frame birdhouse by modifying the house shown in the illustration on p. 47.

Tree-Stump Birdhouse

- Section of a thick tree branch or log
- Board for roof
- Nails (2 penny)
- Small hammer
- Dowel
- Wood glue
- Drill or saw to cut entrance

A section of a log works well for this type of birdhouse. Drill out the inside of the log and an opening through the side for the entrance. Nail on a board for the roof. Use a short section of a dowel for a perch: Drill a hole the size of the dowel below the entrance, place a few drops of glue into the hole, and insert the dowel.

Exploring with Students

Will some birds need a larger house than other birds? Is the opening of your house large enough for a bird to enter yet small enough to keep out cats and other enemies?

A Natural Bird Feeder

1—A Tree for the Birds

Science, Social Studies, Language Arts

Preparation

Read the story beginning on p. 50 to the students as a prelude to the activities that follow.

Tree for Birds

A Natural Bird Feeder

Sam was freezing cold as he walked away from the car, down the dirt trail toward the old mill. Every year during November, an old-time Christmas fair was held at the mill. He pulled his stocking cap snugly over his ears to keep out the Ohio dampness.

"Wow! It's really cold today," he said to his dad, who was behind him on the trail.

There were not many people gathered around the booths outside the mill. Sam ran across the covered bridge, followed by his dad, to see the first booth. A man who was a blacksmith was hammering on a horseshoe he had heated over hot coals. Sam stood and watched for a while, glad for the warmth the coals provided.

"Come on," said Sam's dad. "Let's go to the next booth."

Sam ran over to a large cart that had a red-and-white striped-cloth roof. On top of the cart was a grill where chestnuts were roasting. A man with a nice smile held out a basket, and Sam took one of the nuts and bit into it gingerly.

"Look!" said Sam's dad, pointing to a large fir tree that stood beside the doorway leading into the mill. Sam and his dad walked over to the tree, where two boys were hanging something onto a low branch.

"Would you like to make something for the birds?" asked a lady who stood behind a table beside the tree. She began talking to Sam's dad, telling him how she had grown a large garden of sunflowers and had dried the sunflower heads for the birds. Sam's dad showed him one of the sunflowers and pointed out all the seeds.

"A bird would sure like to find this," said Sam. The lady and his dad helped him tie the sunflower high onto the tree—Sam's dad held him on his shoulders so he could reach the very top.

Back at the table, the lady showed Sam how to spread peanut butter on pinecones using a plastic knife. After he had coated the pinecone with peanut butter, Sam rolled it in a shoebox of birdseed. His dad helped him tie a red piece of yarn around the top of the cone. Sam hung the peanut butter-birdseed pinecone on the tree.

"Birds also like popcorn," the lady told Sam. She helped Sam string popcorn on thread and tie the ends together so it looked like a small wreath. When he added this to the tree, he thought that the tree really looked pretty.

The lady gave him a piece of holly. "This is for you, not the birds!" she said as Sam and his dad left and went into the mill.

Inside the mill, lots of people were wandering around. A man at the door handed Sam and his dad each a small bag. The bags were made out of muslin, and on the front of each bag was a picture of the mill. The bags were filled with cornmeal that had been ground at the mill.

"We can make cornmeal muffins when we get home," Sam's dad told him. Sam was glad that his dad liked to cook, and corn muffins certainly sounded good. Sam wished that he had one right now.

Sam and his dad walked around the mill and saw lots of things for sale. There were dried flowers and leaves for potpourris, stuffed Santas, and all kinds of Christmas decorations. Sam's dad bought two glasses of cider, but when they tasted it, it was cold, and they asked the man to warm it a bit more.

After drinking their cider, Sam and his dad headed out of the mill. Sam smiled when he saw the tree. Lots of sunflowers, peanut butter-birdseed pinecones, and bundles had been hung for the birds.

"That tree is for the birds!" joked his dad as they walked past. The lady who had helped them make the bird ornaments smiled and waved, and they began walking down the path toward their car. A ways down the road, Sam turned around and looked back at the mill. He could see steam from the blacksmith, could still faintly smell the chestnuts, and could see, behind the shapes of many people, the outline of the Christmas tree for the birds.

Activities
1. Obtain a tree that students can decorate for the birds with some of the treats for birds that Sam makes in the story, or with treats students have seen or want to make.
2. Read to students *Night Tree* (1991) by Eve Bunting. In this warm story, a family goes to the forest to decorate a Christmas tree for the animals in the woods.

3. The students may not be familiar with cornmeal and will be interested in tasting it in a bread or cookie. The following cookie recipe comes from *Recipes with Lanterman's Mill Flour and Meal: Stone Ground by Water Power*, distributed by Mill Creek Park in Youngstown, Ohio.

Cornmeal Cookies
Makes 3 dozen

1 cup butter	2 teaspoons lemon juice
1 cup sugar	1½ cups flour
2 eggs	1 cup cornmeal

1. Cream butter, sugar, and eggs.
2. Add lemon juice and mix well.
3. Add flour and cornmeal, and mix to form a soft dough.
4. Refrigerate for 2 hours.
5. Divide dough in half, and roll to a thickness of ⅛ inch.
6. Cut with cookie cutter.
7. Bake 10–12 minutes at 350º F on a greased cookie sheet.

Exploring with Students

Would other animals in the woods want to eat these treats for birds? What else could you hang on the tree for our forests animal friends? Would orange or grapefruit halves make good baskets to fill with raisins, pieces of bread, or birdseed?

Mill Bag

The Wind Blows

1—Weather Vanes

Science, Social Studies, Language Arts, Art

Preparation

Weather vanes are interesting and charming, as well as practical. Talk with the students about the importance of being able to predict the weather. Explain that early American farmers looked to their weather vanes turning in the wind as an immediate weather report.

Weather vanes have a simple design so that they can be seen easily and distinguished from a distance. The design often reflects the life of its creator. For example, in seacoast villages, one sees images of ships, whales, and gulls on weather vanes. In farming communities, pigs, horses, and sheep are common images. Typically, weather vanes are carved from wood, or molded, cut, or cast from metal. Wood weather vanes are painted to protect them from the weather. Most metal weather vanes are not painted.

Show the students a weather vane or photographs of weather vanes. Explain that the weather vane rests on a rod that allows it to turn as the wind blows.

✄ ✄ ✄

In the activity that follows, involve students in creating a weather vane from wood or cardboard. (Cardboard would be for a design; the wood version could actually be used.)

Use of precut wood with holes drilled (if needed) is advised for younger students. Older students may enjoy cutting and drilling their own wood. This should be done under adult supervision only and after students have been made aware of safety precautions they must take.

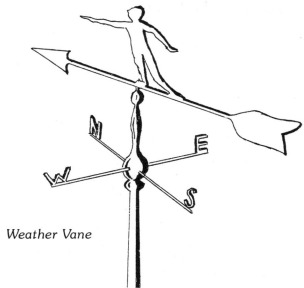

Weather Vane

Each Student Needs

Wood Weather Vane

- Paper and pencil
- Sheet of plywood
- Black marker

- Coping saw
- Thin dowel
- Drill with drill bit (slightly larger in diameter than the dowel)

Cardboard Weather Vane

- Paper and pencil
- Sheet of cardboard
- Black marker
- Scissors
- Drinking straw

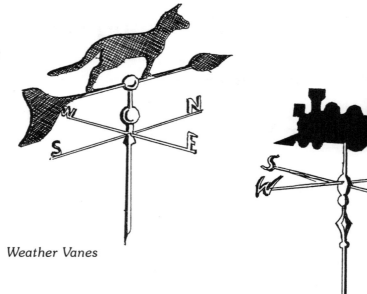

Weather Vanes

Have Each Student

1. On paper, draw a pattern for a weather vane.
2. Cut out the pattern and lay it on a sheet of cardboard or plywood.
3. Using a marker, trace the pattern onto the cardboard or plywood.
4. With a saw (for the wood) or scissors (for the cardboard), cut out the weather vane.
5. Drill or cut a 1- to 2-inch deep hole into the bottom of the wooden weather vane. For the cardboard version, create a socket by rolling a 2-inch long and 1-inch wide piece of heavy construction paper around the straw (or dowel) tightly but not so tight that it stops movement. Glue or tape the end of the strip to hold it in rolled shape. With scissors cut two small slits about ¼-inch deep on bottom of weather vane and insert the socket. Glue into place. The dowel (or straw) should fit loosely into the hole (or socket), so the weather vane can rotate freely.
6. Insert a thin dowel or a straw into the hole.
7. Take the weather vane outside and observe what happens.

Exploring with Students

Can the shape of your weather vane pattern be easily recognized from a distance? On what type of building could you mount your weather vane? Would your weather vane complement a barn, a boathouse, a cabin, or another type of building?

Extending Ideas

1. Weather Vane Game: Have students form a circle, and have one student stand at the center to play the weather vane. Give compasses to some of the students in the circle (every third student, depending on how many compasses are available). One student in the circle calls out "Wind!" The student at the center spins around with one arm outstretched rigidly and pointing. The student who called out "Wind!" now calls out "Calm!" The student at the center immediately stops and stands very still, pointing. The students with the compasses guess which direction the student at the center is pointing. The first student who guesses correctly goes to the center, and the compasses are passed to the right. Repeat the game until every student has had a turn at the center. (Some students may need help guessing the correct direction so they can have a turn playing the weather vane.)

Metal Sculptures

1—Magnetic Creations

Science, Art, Social Studies

Preparation

In the yards of many small towns across the United States, one often sees metal sculptures. Some are sculptures of people, and others are sculptures with no distinguishable shape. All are intriguing, and some incite the observer to knock on the door and talk to the artist who made such an interesting sculpture.

Creating Sculptures at the Sante Fe Children's Museum

Have an industrial magnet and a handful of metal nuts available. Ask a student to place several nuts on the magnet. What happens? Why? Have students add nuts until they have created a sculpture they like, or until the sculpture collapses because it has become unbalanced or too tall. What causes the sculpture to collapse? Have students brainstorm sculpture ideas and experiment with stacking the nuts to create these sculptures. Students will learn some basic laws of physics and properties of magnets during this process.

∅ ∅ ∅

In the activity that follows, involve students in creating their own metal sculptures.

Each Group Needs

- Industrial magnets (available at electrical supply stores)
- Nuts of various sizes
- Sheet of steel, 6 inches wide by $\frac{1}{16}$ to $\frac{1}{4}$ inch thick (a convenient length, such as that of a classroom table)
- Pieces of steel to cover the tops of magnets
- Spiral notebook and pencil

Have Each Group

Before the activity, place the sheet of steel on a table. Lay the magnets sideways on the steel, about 12 inches apart. On top of each magnet, place a small piece of steel that just covers the magnet (to disperse the magnetic force).

1. Stack the nuts into various formations on the magnet.
2. Record observations during the construction process.
3. Share observations with other groups.

Exploring with Students

How many nuts can you stack before the stack topples? Can you construct a base to support more nuts? How does the magnet hold together the nuts, which do not directly touch it?

Extending Ideas

1. Involve students in discovering and exploring some basic properties of magnets. Give each student or pair of students a magnet and several objects, some that can be picked up by the magnet, such as paper clips, nuts, bolts; and others that cannot, such as plastic objects. Have students try to pick up the objects. Have them fold a piece of paper in half and list on one side the objects that are attracted to the magnet, and on the other side the objects that are not. Have students formulate conclusions about magnets based on this information.
2. Have one student pose as a sculpture while the class quickly sketches the student, with a time limit of three minutes. Give each student a chance to pose.
3. Have students use clay to sculpt one another (see illustrations on p. 57).

Posed Child

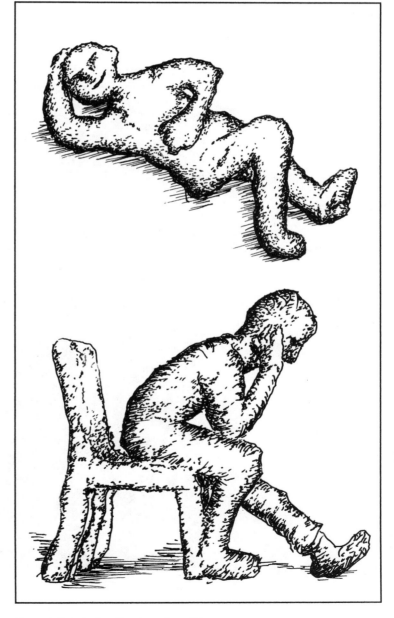

Posed Students Sculpted in Clay

Scarecrows

1—Scarecrows That Keep Crows Away

Social Studies, Art, Science, Language Arts

Preparation

Scarecrows are intriguing to students because they are fun and have lots of personality! Scarecrows are more than this, though; they have played an important role in society. Throughout history, many people have been dependent on the corn and grain grown in their fields. Flocks of crows have destroyed entire fields, leaving families to starve.

Scarecrow

Scarecrows come in many shapes and sizes; some are more effective than others at scaring away crows. People began constructing scarecrows about 2,500 years ago. Drawings and writings describing these ancient scarecrows have been discovered. Through the years, scarecrows have been created by carving wood statues (carved witches in Germany), hanging groups of rags and bones on a pole to blow and clack in the wind, and making hay figures with gourds, pumpkins, turnips, buckets, mops, brooms, and stuffed sacks or rawhide for heads.

In some fields, boys and men acted as scarecrows. They would run at the crows, flapping their hands and throwing stones, or banging pieces of wood together to make a loud noise. Some composed chants to frighten the crows, which they sang as they walked through the fields.

The Scarecrow Book (1980) by Dale Ferguson and James Giblin tells about the use of scarecrows historically. All the scarecrows mentioned above are creative, but do they scare away crows? Throughout history, people have worked to invent effective scarecrows. For example, the Zuni Native Americans had a problem with large flocks of crows and would hold scarecrow building contests. One scarecrow looked like an old woman, with a basket on her back and a rattle in her hand. Another had a horse tail for hair and a long red rag that flapped in the wind for a tongue.

Other scarecrows do not resemble what we consider to be traditional scarecrows. One might see a giant crow with eyes that glow and a metal beak that brightly reflects the sunlight. A farmer in New England is said to have trapped 20 crows and recorded their terrified cries. He played the recording loudly in his field, and very few crows returned to feast on his corn!

∅   ∅   ∅

In the activity that follows, challenge students to design and construct a scarecrow that will successfully scare away crows. As a class, brainstorm how to construct scarecrows that will scare the crows. Ideas might include using reflectors, lights, noise, and movement. Encourage them to be creative. On a large sheet of butcher paper, record students' ideas. Some students will want to begin with a traditional scarecrow body stuffed with straw and then add their creative adaptations, while some will want to design unique and unusual scarecrows (such as a pole with rags that blow in the wind and bones that clack). Emphasize that a scarecrow does not have to look like a person. For young students, it may be more appropriate to design and build a scarecrow as a class.

Traditional Scarecrow Body

Each Group Needs
- Old clothing (shirt, pants, hat, scarf, gloves, boots, belt, suspenders, etc.—inexpensive, colorful clothing is available at thrift shops)
- Shredded newspaper, hay, or straw
- "Head" (pumpkin, mop, or bucket; or stuffed pillowcase, burlap sack, or panty hose; etc.)
- Safety pins
- Tempera paints

- Paintbrushes
- Box or chair for scarecrow to sit on; or a wood stand, hat rack, or coat rack
- Rope or strong twine
- "Junk" materials (optional; see below)

Have Each Group

1. Design a scarecrow that will scare crows.
2. Button the shirt, and pin the tail of the buttoned shirt inside the pants (pinning at the front, back, and sides). Stuff the shirt and pants with newspaper, hay, or straw.
3. Add the head by placing it on top of the torso.
4. Add boots, a tie, a hat, and other clothing, as well as noise makers, reflectors, and other "junk" materials. For example, a soda can containing a few pebbles, hung by a thin piece of elastic around a scarecrow's neck, will blow in the wind and make a noise that scares crows. Bells attached to long banners on a hat will also blow in the wind and make noise. Reflectors might be used for eyes, and large bolts or pieces of pipe are shiny and make noise if hung so they can hit each other in the blowing wind.
5. Tie the scarecrow to a stand (such as a coat rack) using rope or strong twine, or sit the scarecrow on a box or chair, arranging it like it would appear standing or sitting in a field.

Exploring with Students

Are you adding junk to your scarecrow which provides noise, motion, or color? What makes your scarecrow unique?

Extending Ideas

1. Discuss the value of having crows in a cornfield. Ask the students whether or not crows serve any purpose. Help them understand that some crows are helpful because they eat corn borers and other damaging insects.
2. Have each group of students write a guidebook describing the steps they used to build the scarecrow. Have students write the directions clearly, so anyone reading them could build the scarecrow.
3. Have young students pretend to be scarecrows, and create a dance set to music. Ask students how a scarecrow would dance if it could move.
4. Guide the students in researching crows. Different varieties of crows live in different parts of the United States (e.g., common crows live in the East and some parts of the West; northwestern crows live near tidewaters). For illustrations of various crows and more specific information, refer students to *A Guide to Field Identification: Birds of North America* (1966) by Chandler S. Robbins, Bertel Brunn, and Herbert S. Zim.
5. With the students, discuss the old adage "birds of a feather flock together." Ask them what this expression means and if they find it to be true in their lives and in the world around them. Involve students in illustrating this expression. Ask students to name other animals that travel and live together in groups. Why do they do this?

Hobby Animals

1—A Riding Toy

Social Studies, Art, Emotional and Social Development, Music

Preparation

In every part of the world, people depend on animals for transportation and to carry their supplies. In the United States, people use horses and mules, in Peru donkeys and llamas, in Africa elephants, and in Asia camels.

Explain to the students that they will be creating a traditional hobby horse or a hobby animal of choice portraying an animal that is traditionally used in another country. Have students watch as you stuff a large sock with newspaper. Show them how to stuff different areas to sculpt the shape of a head. With the students, brainstorm ideas for the mane, eyes, ears, and so on.

✄ ✄ ✄

In the activity that follows, involve students in making their own hobby animals.

Each Student Needs
- Large sock
- Buttons, yarn, yarn needle, and other decorative materials
- Newspaper
- Masking tape
- Wood dowel, ¾ inch diameter by 36 inches long; or broom or mop handle

Have Each Student
1. Stuff a sock with newspaper to make an animal's head.
2. Add ears, shaggy hair, mane, eyes, and any other desired details.
3. Stitch on a yarn mouth (see burlap stitchery in colorful cloth, p. 154, for basic stitch).
4. Place the dowel or handle into the sock opening. Arrange the newspaper around the dowel or handle to form a neck.
5. Tape the end of the sock tightly to the dowel or handle.

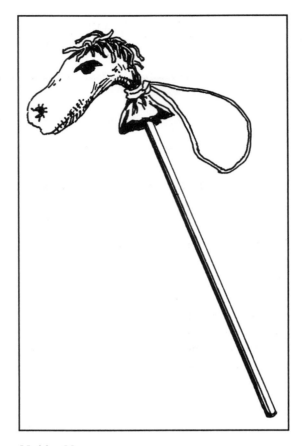

Hobby Horse

Exploring with Students

What animal are you making? What materials can you use for its ears, hair, eyes, and characteristic features?

Extending Ideas

1. Involve students in singing the following song, "Hobby Animal." Have them pretend that they are traveling on their hobby animals to the places in the song.

HOBBY ANIMAL

I'm rid- ing my hob- by an- i- mal; It can
be an- y an- i- mal at all. I'm trav- el- ling to man- y
dif- ferent plac- es; On an- i- mals, big and small.

Fine

1. It can be a li- on in the jun- gle; Or a
2. It can be a hip- po in the riv- er; Or a
3. It can be a griz- zly in the moun- tains; Or an

cam- el on the des- ert sand.
drag- on in a mag- ic place.
ea- gle soar- ing high and low.

It can be a don- key in a can- yon; Or a
It can be an ele- phant in the cir- cus; Or a
It can be a sea- horse in the o- cean; Or a

D.C. al Fine

cow on a gras- sy range land.
horse in a stee- ple- chase race.
dino- saur from long - a- go.

Wooden Ship Ornaments

1—Ship Figureheads

Social Studies, Art, Science, Language Arts

Figureheads at the Art Institute of Chicago

Preparation

During the 1700s and 1800s, wood trading and whaling ships sailed from East Coast towns in the United States to every port in the world. At the prow of many ships was a carved ornament called a figurehead. A ship could be identified by its figurehead, which was thought to bring good luck. The figureheads were carved from blocks of white pine and fastened together with dowels.

Show the students pictures of figureheads from old ships. Explain that the woodcarvers often carved a female figure to fasten to the prow of a ship because ships are often referred to as being female in gender. Sometimes the image of a daughter or wife was carved; other ships had the image of a famous person. Some original figureheads are housed in museums, such as the Art Institute of Chicago, but few remain. Many were lost in shipwrecks. When wood ships were replaced with ships made of steel, the era of figureheads came to an end.

⌁ ⌁ ⌁

In the activity that follows, involve students in sculpting model figureheads. Ask students to imagine a figurehead they would sculpt if they had owned one of the wood ships at some time between the pre-Revolutionary days and the Civil War.

Each Student Needs

- Baker's dough
    Mix and chill: 4 cups flour, 1 cup salt, and 1½ cups water. This is enough for several children each to make a small figurehead.
- Tempera paints
- Paintbrushes
- Optional: Toothpicks, plastic knives, cookie sheet

Have Each Student

1. Sculpt a model figurehead for a ship. Think about what the ship may have looked like, what kinds of goods it may have transported, and where it may have traveled. No tools are need to work with the dough. Details can be etched into it using toothpicks or plastic knives. Dough will dry in several days or can be baked at 300° in oven for 1½ hours.
2. When the clay is dry, paint the figurehead with tempera paints.
3. Share the figurehead with a classmate.

Exploring with Students

Are you using your fingers to sculpt the figurehead, or are you also using tools such as a toothpick and a plastic knife? If you were to mount your figurehead on a ship the size of a shoe box, would the figurehead be large or small in relation to the size of the ship?

Sculpted Figurehead

Extending Ideas

1. Have the students exchange figureheads and pretend they are archaeologists who have just found the figureheads. Ask the students: What can you tell from your find? What type of ship might have displayed this figurehead? Who might the figure be? Where might the ship have gone, and what might it have carried? Have students write their ideas on a sheet of paper and give the writing to the figurehead's creator.

   Have the students read what has been written about their sculpture and discuss whether or not the archaeological deductions are true based on what they had in mind when they sculpted the figure. Discuss with students how errors of deduction sometimes occur in archaeology. Sometimes archaeologists have a lot of information on which to base their findings, but other times they do not. They do the best they can with the information available, then clarify their understanding with additional information gathered from other findings.

Etched in Bone

1—Scrimshaw

Science, Social Studies, Art, Language Arts

Preparation

Have photographs of scrimshaw or actual scrimshaw items available for the students to examine. Tell them that if they had taken a whaling journey during the 1700s or 1800s, they might have been away from home for up to three years—a long time to be at sea. Many men and boys who went on whaling expeditions carved designs into whales' teeth, walrus tusks, and pieces of whalebone. They rubbed soot into the etching to highlight the design, and then polished the piece of bone or tooth.

Involve the students in thinking about what it might have been like to be away from home for a long time on a whaling vessel. Good books to read about whaling trips are *Whaling Days* (1993) by Carol Carrick and *The Story of the New England Whalers* (1982) by R. Conrad Stein.

℘ ℘ ℘

In the activity that follows, have students try the process of etching a design and highlighting it with soot, using a plastic bottle. Before beginning the activity, brainstorm with students about the types of designs that sailors might have etched. Ship and whale designs were common. Other designs included trees, flowers, and famous people of that day, such as a U.S. president.

Scrimshaw

Each Student Needs

- White, plastic bottle (small, white bleach detergent or clear plastic pop bottles)
- Yarn needle, nail, or safety pin
- White saucer
- Candle
- Match
- Paper towel
- Dish detergent
- Paper and pencil

Have Each Student

1. Think of a design, and sketch it on a piece of paper. Plan where to etch it on the bottle.
2. Draw the design on the bottle very lightly, using a pencil, so the design can be wiped off or changed if necessary.
3. Carefully and under adult supervision, etch the design into the bottle using a needle, nail, or safety pin. Be sure the etching is rough to the touch and not just indents. (Soot will hold better.)
4. Light a candle in a stable candle holder. Hold a white saucer over the flame until carbon forms on the bottom of the saucer.

   Safety Note: Depending on the age of the student, the teacher may need to do step 4. For older children who are holding their own saucers, warn them to tilt the saucer so their fingers are on the lower edge. The heat from the candle flame will flow up the tilted saucer and away from their fingers.
5. Using your thumb, rub carbon into the etching.
6. Polish the bottle by wiping it clean with a paper towel moistened with a few drops of dish detergent.

Exploring with Students

What design are you etching? If you are etching a ship, is it detailed to resemble the whaling ships of this time period?

Extending Ideas

1. Have students write a story to accompany the etching. Have the students imagine that they are on a whaling vessel. Students may want to research whales and whaling expeditions. Display the writings and the bottles.
2. Have students investigate present-day whaling activities. Are whales endangered?

Dolls

1—Dolls Can Represent Who We Are

Social Studies, Art, Language Arts

Preparation

Throughout history, our dolls have reflected who we are. Some of the dolls of the first pioneers in the United States during the seventeenth through nineteenth centuries were made from the natural materials around them. Dolls were made from stumps, corncobs, cornhusks, and apples. Many European dolls were refined, and makers often dressed them in the clothes worn by children and adults during this time period. Dolls represent the culture of their makers. In Central America, some dolls have baskets on their heads, representing one way that Maya Native Americans carry their goods.

The dolls of Native American tribes are good examples of how dolls model humans through time. Their dolls were miniature models of different Native American groups, regarding their hairstyles, the clothing they wore, and the accessories they valued. Share with students the book *Dolls & Toys of Native America: A Journey Through Childhood* (1995) by Don McQuiston and Debra McQuiston, a beautiful collection of Native American dolls. It is enjoyable and intriguing to see how closely dolls resembled the children who played with them. One Eskimo doll dressed in the traditional sealskin hunting suit resembled the clothing worn by Eskimo hunters. Another Eskimo doll with a baby riding on the mother's back, peeking out of the mother's cozy fur coat, shows a traditional Eskimo baby who rode on the mother's back, covered by her parka for warmth. A doll played with by children of the Crow tribe had many white beads sewn onto her dress. These beads represented the elk teeth that were traditionally sewn onto the women's dresses. Some Native American dolls combined cornhusks and decorative clothing (see illustration, p. 70).

Encourage students to think about who they are and how they live. Explain that archaeologists who find old dolls can tell a lot about the people who made them—hairstyle, the clothing they wore, and the materials that were available in the environment. Ask students: If a future archaeologist were to find one of your dolls, what would the archaeologist think about your life? Have students think of a specific doll, such as a Barbie or GI Joe, and guide them in discussing the message that the doll sends. Discuss how the doll might send a message about society, but that the message might not necessarily reflect its owner. Ask students: If you were to make a doll that reflects who you are, what would it look like?

✐ ✐ ✐

In the activity that follows, involve the students in creating a simple doll that represents who they are. Or, as an alternate activity, have students create a doll that represents a time period of long ago (e.g., a pioneer doll, a Native American doll, etc.).

Each Student Needs

- 12-by-12-inch squares of plain-colored cotton fabric for doll's body (various shades for different skin colors)
- Pieces of fabric for clothing
- Marker, pen, or pencil
- Straight pins
- Scissors
- Thread
- Needles or sewing machine
- Cotton batting
- Beads, buttons, yarn, and other decorative materials
- Acrylic or tempera paints
- Paintbrushes

Have Each Student

1. Pin together two squares of fabric, pinning around the edges and inside the square.

2. Using a marker, pen, or pencil, draw the outline of a person in a "gingerbread man" shape. Add several pins inside the shape to secure.

Leather Native American Doll

3. Cut out the shape, cutting through both pieces of fabric.

4. Sew together the two pieces of fabric, around the outside edge of the shape, by hand or using a sewing machine. Leave a 3-inch space open on the side of the shape through which to insert batting. Turn the shape inside out so the seam will not show.

   Safety Note: Handle the needle carefully because it is sharp, and keep your fingers away from the sewing machine needle.

5. Push batting into the arms, legs, body, head, and neck of the figure. Close the opening through which the batting was inserted using needle and thread.

6. Using fabric, dress the figure. For example, make a simple dress by cutting a hole in a rectangle of fabric. Slip the fabric over the doll's head, and tie it in place using a piece of yarn around the waist (see illustration, p. 71). Sew together the sides of the dress, leaving openings for the arms. To make pants, cut the dress between the legs and sew together the fabric. Tie a piece of yarn around the waist to create the look of a shirt, a belt, and pants.

Clothing for Doll

7. Add yarn for hair by sewing short pieces onto the head.
8. Carefully paint eyes, a nose, a mouth, and cheeks using acrylic or tempera paints.

Exploring with Students

Are you creating a doll that represents you, or a doll that represents a different time period? What message does your doll send about you, or about the different time period?

Extending Ideas

1. Encourage the students to share their dolls with classmates. Divide the class into groups of future archaeologists. Have groups exchange dolls and examine them carefully. What message does each doll send about the person who created it? Students will enjoy hearing someone interpret their creation.

2. Read to students the book *The Legend of the Bluebonnet* (1983) by Tomie dePaola. This is a lovely story of a young Comanche girl who threw her beloved doll into the fire as a sacrifice for her people.

3. Just as dolls represent the people that make them, so do doll houses. Historically, doll houses were created as models of houses in the community, or in the case of the pioneers, as models of homesteading households. Talk with students about how doll houses were built from small sticks or branches to resemble the log homes of their owners. Some were Victorian in design, and others took the shape of teepees, carpeted with animal furs. Challenge the students to select a community and time period and create a house that depicts how people lived during that era. Have students construct the doll houses using wood, cardboard boxes, clay bricks (see activity for making adobe houses on p. 39), and even straw or sheets of bark.

2—Kachina Dolls

Art, Social Studies

Preparation

Some dolls do not resemble the people of a culture but reflect the culture itself in various ways. The first doll given to infant Hopi girls (and in some villages, infant boys) is a flat kachina doll. Read to students the following account of two doll makers who work hard at creating the traditional kachina dolls of their cultures.

Kachina

After the story, talk with the students about kachina dolls, and then share with them the information that follows about artists who make different types of dolls.

Making a Kachina

Ronald Jean is a Hopi Native American. He has crafted kachina dolls from cottonwood for more than 30 years. The kachina doll is a carved representation of a kachina dancer. Ronald carves figures to resemble dancers at a Hopi ceremony. Some have eagle feathers, and others have jaws and teeth like a bear. One of his kachinas wears a black-and-white striped outfit and sits in a tree branch eating watermelon. Ronald explains that this striped kachina is the Hopi clown.

Ronald lives in Shiprock, New Mexico, with his wife, Julie. Julie is Navajo. She paints the kachinas after Ronald carves them. They enjoy making the kachina dolls. They take some of their dolls to trading posts, where people buy kachinas for their homes.

Ronald and Julie live close to Julie's family. They raise sheep, goats, and other animals.

Ronald Jean in His Workshop

Activities

1. Show the students photographs of kachina dolls. Explain to them that the original kachina dolls were flat dolls. The dolls were given to girls when they were born, to newly married women, and to women who desired to have children. With time, kachina dolls became more elaborate in form and more intricate in detail.

2. It will be difficult for students to make a replica of an authentic flat kachina (even the flat kachinas had faces from dancers in the ceremonies) or a full-figured kachina if they do not know about the Hopi ceremonies and dancers. Share with students the book *Kachina Dolls: Form and Function in Hopi Tithu* (1990), published by the Museum of Northern Arizona. If there is someone in your community who has a kachina doll, invite that person to bring the doll to class for students to examine.

3—Cloth Dolls from Guatemala

Art and Social Studies

Preparation

Small cloth dolls are common in Central America. Read to students the following account of a Guatemalan doll maker, and then share with them the steps she uses to create a small fabric doll (see illustrations pp. 75–76).

A Doll Maker

Francisca Perez DePayola is a weaver and doll maker who lives in the village of Antigua, Guatemala. Francisca is 58 years old and has 6 children and 18 grandchildren. She has made dolls for many years. She weaves the strips of cloth for the dolls' clothing. Sometimes, for variety, she uses fabric that her friends have woven. Francisca sews the dolls at night while lying in bed. She goes to the village market early every morning to sell her dolls. Some days the business is good, and other days the business is very slow.

Francisca also makes and sells wreaths, bags, clothing, wall hangings, and purses. Her husband makes the wire frames for the wreaths. (He also wraps fabric around thin wires for the dolls' arms and legs.) It takes about a week to make a wreath. Francisca is proud of her work. She says, "Every doll is unique, and every doll maker is unique."

Francisca Holding Wreaths

The following drawings (below and p. 76) illustrate the steps Francisca follows as she creates her small, fabric dolls.

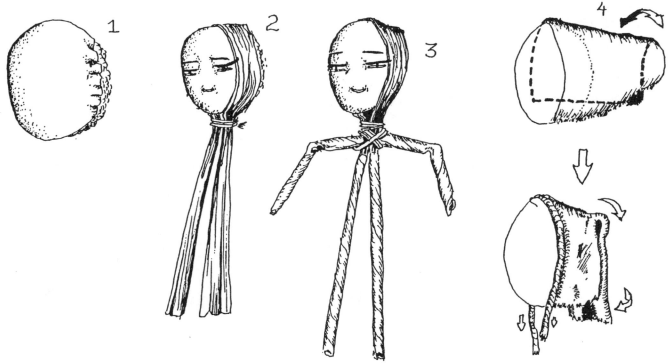

Steps 1-4 for Making Guatemalan Dolls

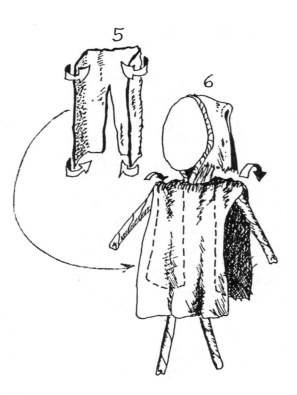

Steps 5-7 for Making Guatemalan Dolls

In Guatemala, artists who make these fabric dolls also string them on bead necklaces, mount them on fabric-covered cardboard circles to create wreaths like Francisca's, and sell them in small bundles.

Activities

African women in Ghana make a doll called an Akua-ba doll. (To create a similar African doll, see pp. 120–21.)

Guatemalan Necklace

Puppets from Long Ago

1—Puppets on a Stick

Social Studies, Art, Language Arts, Music

Preparation

Throughout history, children have been enchanted with puppets. Have a collection of various puppets (hand, string, and stick) available for the students to manipulate and discuss. Ask students: What makes a puppet engaging? How would you describe the personalities of the puppets?

∅ ∅ ∅

In the activity that follows, involve students in creating a stick puppet similar to those children made more than 150 years ago.

Each Student Needs

- Baker's dough
    Mix and chill: 4 cups flour, 1 cup salt, and 1½ cups water. Each recipe batch will make three puppets.
- Yarn or ribbon
- Straw
- Dowel
- Patterns (photocopies, pp. 79-80)
- Cookie sheet and oven
- Pieces of fabric
- Scissors
- Needle and thread
- Glue
- Name card (with student's name)
- Paint and paintbrushes

Have Each Student

1. Divide the dough into four small balls for the arms and legs, one large ball for the body, and a medium-sized ball for the head. Sculpt the head, body, two arms, and two legs.

2. Using a straw, poke holes for the joints (at the top of each arm and leg, and in the body where the arms and legs will be fastened).

3. Slip a dowel through the body (from bottom to top) and halfway into the head. If necessary, reshape the body after inserting the dowel.

4. Place the body parts on a cookie sheet and bake at 350° F until the underside is golden brown (about 1½ hours). Air drying at room temperature for several days is also acceptable. (If baking several puppets together, write names on the dowel.)

5. Using pieces of yarn or ribbon, tie on the arms and legs.

6. Sew on clothing, and add hair (yarn), accessories, and details (see pp. 70–71 for a simple dress pattern).

Exploring with Students

Are you inventing a puppet character, or are you creating a likeness of someone you know (or a famous person or a book character)? Have you added clothing and accessories appropriate to your puppet's personality?

Extending Ideas

1. For a fun, creative movement activity, have students pretend that they are puppets on a stick. Teach the students the song (see p. 81), "I'm a Puppet Made of Clay." After singing the song once, have students take turns thinking of a puppetlike movement, such as moving their arms up and down, clapping, hopping on one foot, turning their heads from side to side, or kicking out their legs. Repeat the song as many times as desired, performing a different movement each time. Have students try to perform the movements "in time" with the music, and try to combine two or more movements.

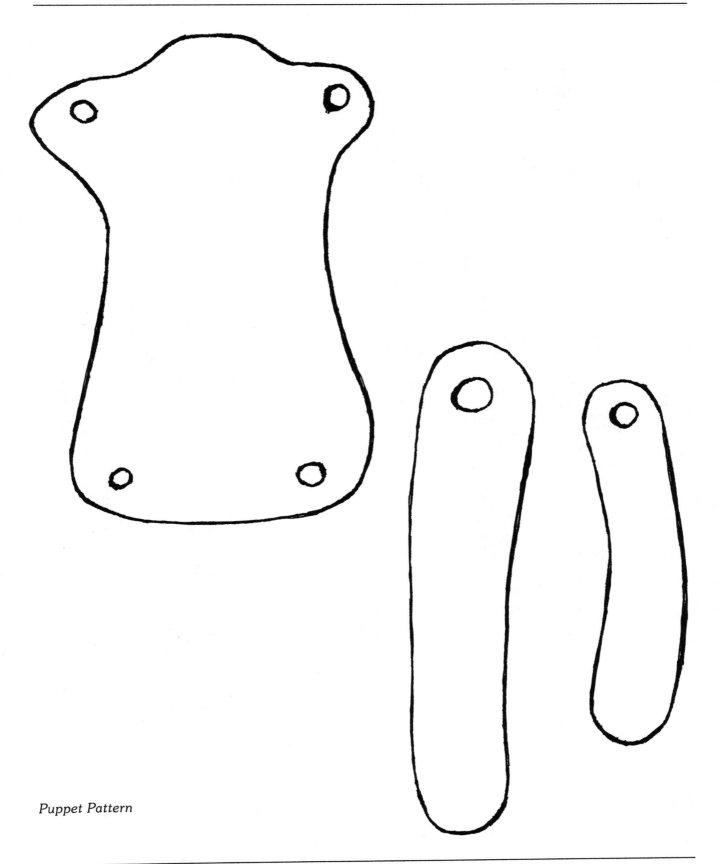

Puppet Pattern

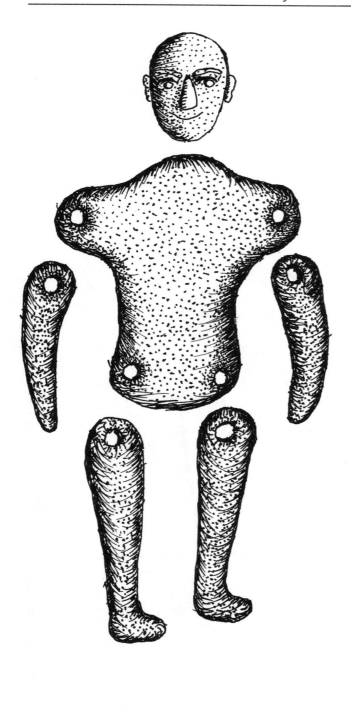

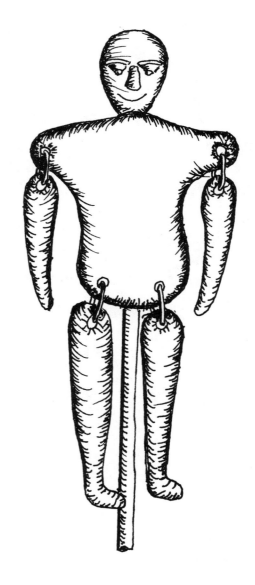

Puppet Assembly

I'M A PUPPET MADE OF CLAY

I'm a pup- pet made of clay; I like to sing and dance all day. You can

hold my stick, and I'll do a trick! I'm a pup- pet made of clay.

From the Earth

Stories on Stone

1—Rock Art

Social Studies, Art, Language Arts

Preparation

Through the ages in all parts of the world, ancient peoples left messages on rocks, called pictographs. Some etched them in stone, and others painted them on the sides of caves in places from the Mtoko Cave in Zimbabwe to the canyons of Utah. Share with students the book *Messages on Stone* (1980) by William Michael Stokes and William Lee Stokes, an excellent resource on ideas communicated on stone. The authors show examples of and explain different groups of symbols used to communicate messages, such as birds, feet and footprints, hands, hunting, insects, animals, plants, shields, water, and weather.

Pictographs

Show the students examples of pictographs from the Native Americans and other peoples of the world. Talk with them about how entire stories can be communicated through fairly simple symbols.

Involve the students in thinking about the similarities between drawing symbols on rocks and writing about an experience or event. Ask students: If you were to record an event from your life using symbols, what would the event be and what symbols would you use to represent your experience? On a sheet of paper, have each student create symbols (using crayons or markers) to tell of an experience they would like to share with a classmate. Have students make a key for the symbols on the back of the paper or on another sheet of paper. Have students exchange papers and read about one another's experiences. Could people communicate as effectively if they drew pictures instead of using words and sentences?

∅ ∅ ∅

In the activity that follows, have students try two methods of making symbols on sandpaper (to simulate the surface of a rock). Although students will not be making symbols on rocks, these processes are similar to those actually used to create pictographs.

Each Student Needs

- Two sheets of sandpaper, any coarseness.
- Black crayon
- Small sponge (damp sponges do not absorb as much paint as dry sponges and are easier to control)
- Black tempera paint
- Paper
- Scissors
- Optional: Pencil
- Optional: Nails, safety glasses
- Optional: Semi-flat surfaced rock

Have Each Student

Drawing Symbols

1. On a sheet of sandpaper, draw a pictograph illustration using the black crayon.
2. Explain the drawing to a classmate.

Splattering Around a Shape

1. On paper, draw a shape, such as an animal or a hand. Cut out the figure.
2. Lay the pattern on a sheet of sandpaper.
3. Dip the sponge into black paint and sponge the paint over and around the pattern.
4. When the paint is dry, carefully lift off the pattern.

Optional: Carving Symbols

1. Have students draw a symbol on their rock with a pencil.
2. After explaining safety precautions of chipping rock, have students carefully use a nail to etch their drawing into the rock.

Exploring with Students

If someone saw your picture, what story would it tell them?

Simple Pictographs

Extending Ideas

1. Involve students in acting out a short skit about an event that may have happened long ago. After the students act out the skit, lead the class in creating symbols to represent what they have just experienced.
2. Challenge the students to think about symbols and signs in their environment that represent various ideas, such as traffic signs, yellow curbs, and handicapped parking spots. Ask students to keep a record in a journal for a few days of the signs and symbols they see. As a class, record the signs and symbols on a chart. Using a simple graph, graph the numbers of each sign and symbol observed.

3. Read to students the book *Talking Walls* (1992) by Margy Burns Knight. This portrays many kinds of walls that contain messages. Knight includes walls such as the Great Wall of China, paintings on the walls of caves, the Western Wall in Jerusalem, cliffs in India, and the Vietnam Veterans Memorial. Discuss these walls with the students and the stories that the walls tell.

4. Murals have decorated walls for thousands of years. Diego Rivera is often recognized for his intriguing political murals on walls in Mexico. Read to students *Diego* (1991) by Jeanette Winter, an interesting children's book about Diego Rivera.

5. Have students paint murals on walls (or large pieces of butcher paper). Assign students a theme, such as famous people who have contributed important ideas and achievements. Have the students work in groups and brainstorm ideas for the mural. Have each student in a group create a portion of the mural on a piece of paper. Have the group piece together the designs to create the mural, thereby giving equal weight to each student's idea. Or, have each group appoint a leader who will involve the group in deciding on the overall design and delegate responsibilities. A third possibility is a combination of these two methods, with a leader helping the group assemble students' ideas into a mural. Have each group discuss how they developed their mural (for example, how they decided on the ideas and whether the group collaboration was successful), and what their design represents.

Mural on Guatemalan Wall

6. Have students make a tile mural using potter's clay. Roll out the clay to fill an 18-by-24-inch wood frame. Scrape a ruler (or other straight edge) across the top of the frame to remove excess clay. Using a pencil tip or other pointed object (such as a nail), sketch a design onto the clay. (See illustration below.) Using a plastic knife, spoon, or other small scoop-shaped object, dig out the clay around the design so the surface of the design is raised above the background. Measure and cut the clay into squares. Cover lightly with a piece of plastic. When the squares are slightly dry (in about one day), lift each tile and scratch a number on the back. Lay the squares back into the frame, and again cover them lightly until they are completely dry (several days). Fire the squares in a kiln, glaze, and fire again. Create a tile inlay in a wall, or frame the tiles and hang them as a picture. (See illustrations, p. 90.)

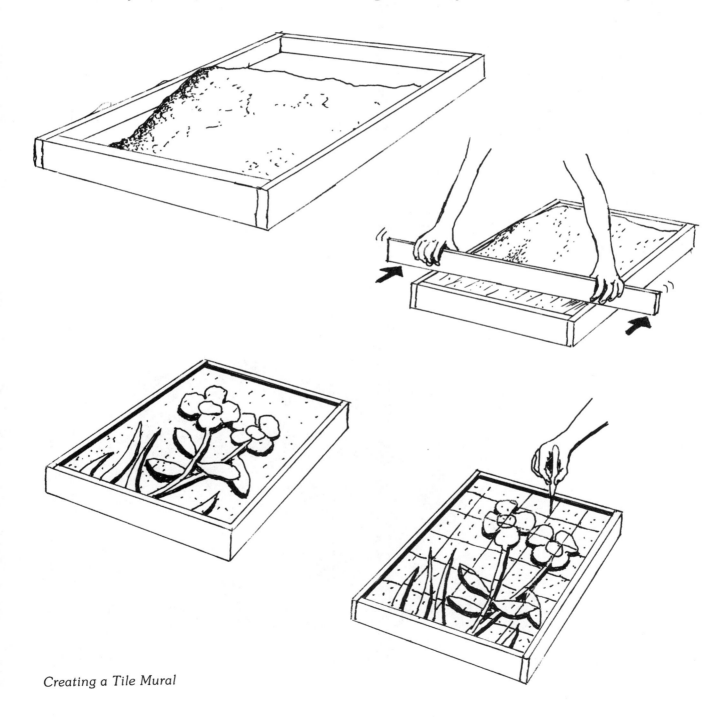

Creating a Tile Mural

Creating a Tile Mural

Tile Mural

Corn

Throughout history, corn has played a significant role in the lives of many peoples. Corn became a symbol of the continuation of life. Corn is used for food and decoration, and the husks made into toys. Wonderful folk art toys and items, such as the corn prosperity doll and the Peruvian donkey, are made from ears of corn and cornhusks.

Corn Seen from a Hogan Window

1—Prosperity Doll

Social Studies, Art

Preparation

Mary "Happi" Trail makes and sells a charming doll made from ears of corn. With each doll, she includes a sign that reads: "Native Americans used corn as a continuation of life. They created abundance by sharing seeds with their white brothers. This corn doll represents the essence of the seeds of prosperity for you, and your surroundings."

Read Mary "Happi" Trail's above thoughts to the students. Discuss her ideas and involve each student in the interpretation.

✿ ✿ ✿

In the activity that follows, involve the students in creating a prosperity doll of their own.

Each Student Needs

- Small gourd
- Black yarn
- Scissors
- Hot glue gun
- Four ears of colored miniature corn
- Black fabric or felt
- Black marker

Have Each Student

1. Lay two ears of corn side by side to make the legs and body. Tie them together at the husks using yarn (see illustration, step 1, p. 93).

2. Lay an ear of corn on each side of the body to make the arms. Tie them to the husks of the body.

3. Glue the gourd to the body to make the head.

    Safety Note: An adult will need to supervise and help with the hot glue gun.

4. Cut pieces of yarn and glue them onto the gourd to make hair.

5. Using a black marker, draw a face on the gourd.

6. Make a simple dress by cutting a rectangle of fabric or felt large enough to wrap as a backward shawl around the top of the doll, and a second rectangle to wrap as a skirt beneath the shawl (see illustrations, steps 2 and 3, pp. 93-94). Fasten the clothing in place by gluing the skirt and shawl together at the seams.

7. Share the doll with a classmate.

Exploring with Students

Would it be helpful if you have a friend hold the ears of corn in place while you tie them together? What does the word *prosperity* mean to you?

Prosperity Doll

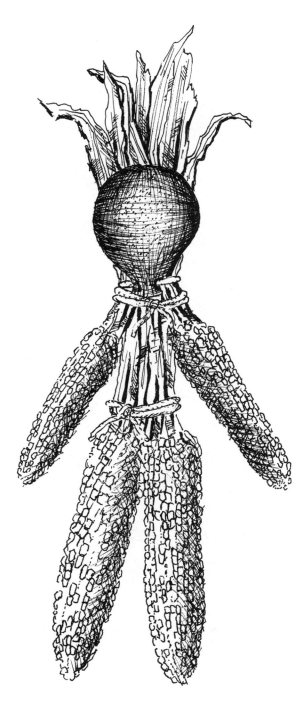

Step 1—Making a Prosperity Doll

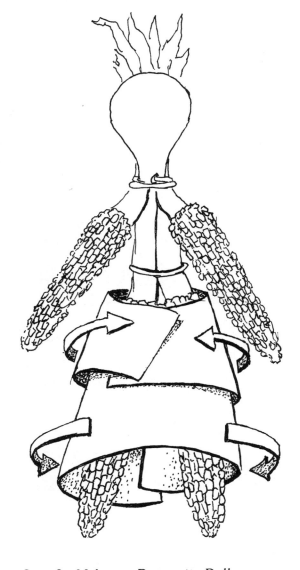

Step 2—Making a Prosperity Doll

Step 3—Making a Prosperity Doll

2—Donkeys from Peru

Social Studies, Art

Preparation

All over the world, animals carry goods from one location to another. The donkey is a popular pack animal.

✍ ✍ ✍

In the activity that follows, involve students in creating a small donkey from a cornhusk, similar to those often sold in Mexico.

Each Student Needs

- Cornhusks
- Scissors
- Black marker
- Yarn or twine
- Pan of water

Have Each Student

1. Soak cornhusks until they are soft and pliable.

2. For the legs of the donkey, cut two rectangles (about 1½ inch by 3 inches) of husk and roll them into cylinders 3 inches long. Tie short (2-3 inches) pieces of yarn or twine around the ends of the husks. Each husk will become two legs when it is folded in half.

3. Cut another 1½-by-3-inch rectangle for the body. Roll it into a cylinder. One end of the body will become the head.

4. Cut and roll a 1½-by-1½-inch square of husk. Bend it slightly at the middle. This husk will become the ears. To make the head, fold ½ inch of the body husk over the ears and tie with yarn or twine (see illustration).

5. Fold each leg husk in half over the body husk and tie with yarn or twine beneath the body.

6. Add a 1-by-2-inch piece of husk to make a blanket and tie with yarn or twine.

7. Add eyes with a black marker.

Cornhusk Donkey

Note: The dimensions given above make a donkey about 2 inches tall. The size of each piece can be increased proportionally to make a larger donkey.

Exploring with Students

What might your donkey carry as it walks through the Andes? Along the streets of a village in Mexico?

3—Paper Ears of Corn

Art, Social Studies

Preparation

Colored corn makes beautiful decorations and captures the mood of a fall day. Mosaic paper ears of corn are a stimulating art project and are almost as colorful as the real thing. Talk with the students about mosaics. Explain that a mosaic is a picture made by piecing together small pieces of glass, tile, paper, or other objects. Have a mosaic or a picture of a mosaic available for the students to examine.

Ø Ø Ø

In the activity that follows, involve students in creating an ear of corn using a mosaic technique. Before beginning, involve the students in helping to cut many tiny squares of red, yellow, orange, dark blue, and brown construction paper. It saves time to cut a strip the full length of the paper, and then cut the strips (several at a time) into small squares.

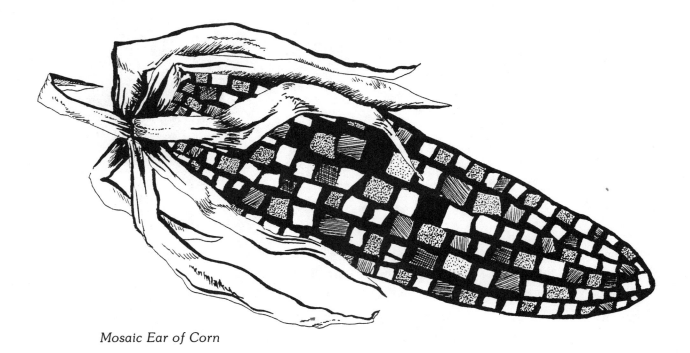

Mosaic Ear of Corn

Each Student Needs

- Construction paper squares: dark blue, yellow, orange, red, and brown
- Black construction paper
- Yellow tissue or crepe paper
- Scissors
- Glue
- Pencil

Have Each Student

1. Draw a large ear of corn on a piece of black construction paper.
2. Cut out the ear of corn.
3. Glue the small colored squares in rows on the ear of corn.
4. Cut husks out of the tissue or crepe paper and glue them to the end of the ear of corn.

Exploring with Students

After you glue on a few rows of squares, can you estimate how many it will take to fill the ear? Are you gluing each square to the black paper, or are you spreading some glue on a section of the ear and then adding the squares?

Extending Ideas

1. Real mosaic pictures are usually made with small squares of ceramic tile. These small squares (tesserae) can be purchased at many craft stores or ordered from art catalogs. Order ceramic tiles for the class, and have students follow the directions for removing the small tiles from the backing. The squares can be used as they are, or broken into other shapes using pincers.

   Have the students draw a picture on a piece of plywood and glue the individual ceramic pieces onto the board. Using a paintbrush or fingers, fill in the spaces between the tesserae using a thick mixture of water and plaster. Let the picture dry, and wipe it clean with a rag.

4—Cornhusk Ristras

Social Studies, Science, Art, Music

Preparation

Many open markets in Arizona, New Mexico, and other areas in the Southwest sell red pepper (chile) strings to hang in a kitchen, a pantry, under a porch, or by a front door. The red chile string is called a ristra (REE-strah). Ristras are made with freshly picked red peppers. Once the chilies have dried, they can be torn off the string and ground to make spice. Many adobe houses have pepper strings for decoration and for use in the kitchen.

⌀ ⌀ ⌀

In the activity that follows, involve the students in making an imitation ristra. Real peppers may be strung, but the oil from peppers can painfully sting eyes, lips, and noses. Cornhusks are a simple substitution.

Each Student Needs

- Dried cornhusks (available at many grocery stores; or husks can be dried by laying them out in a sunny place)
- Bucket of water
- Newspaper
- Scissors
- Twine or yarn
- Yarn needle
- Red berries or red clothing dye
- Paint shirt to protect students' clothing

Have Each Student (or Group of Students)

1. Mix red clothing dye into a bucket of water.
2. Add cornhusks and soak until red.
3. Lay cornhusks on a sheet of newspaper and dry them until they can be handled easily (very wet cornhusks can easily be strung on yarn but will dye students' hands red as they work).
4. String a yarn needle with a piece of yarn about 1 yard long.
5. Tie a large knot at the end of the yarn and thread the husks by pushing the needle through the center of each husk and then pushing the husk toward the knot (the same process as beading).
6. Trim the ends of each husk so they look more like the rounded ends of peppers.
7. Hang the cornhusk string and enjoy a feeling of the Southwest.

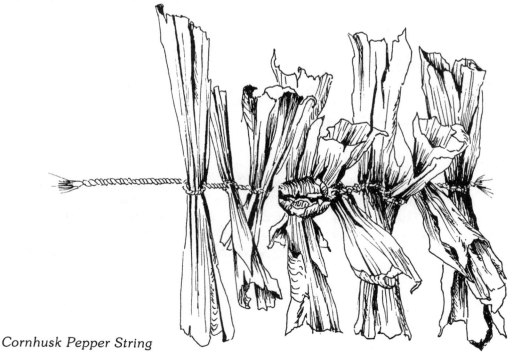

Cornhusk Pepper String

Exploring with Students

Does it help with the stringing if you separate the husks? Are you stringing on more than one husk at a time? Can you arrange the husks on the yarn so that they are pointing in various directions, like a pepper string?

Extending Ideas

1. Ask the students if someone in their home uses recipes that contain hot peppers. Have them bring the recipes to school, and make a class "pepper book" of the various recipes. Have students make a book cover that resembles a pepper. Have a "red-hot tasting day" and try the recipes.

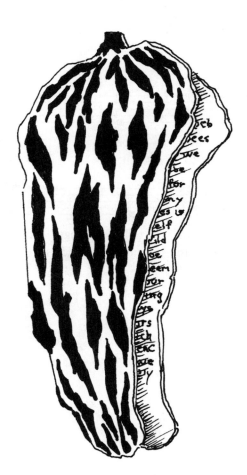

Pepper-Shaped Book

2. Involve the students in singing the song on page 100, "Ristras." (*Ristra* is Spanish for a string of peppers, garlic, onions, etc.) If the students have made cornhusk strings in the activity above, hang them about the room and pretend that you are in a market that sells peppers.

RISTRAS

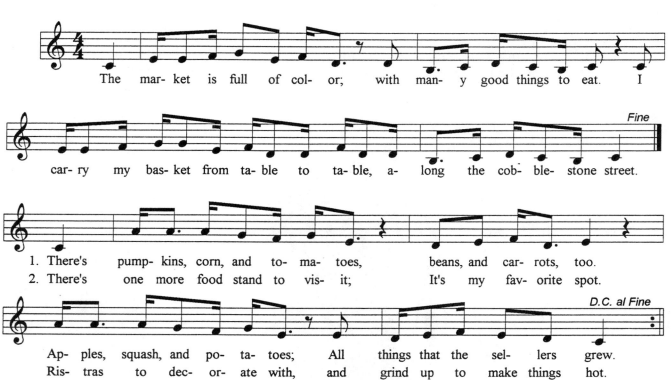

The mar- ket is full of col- or; with man- y good things to eat. I

Fine

car- ry my bas- ket from ta- ble to ta- ble, a- long the cob- ble- stone street.

1. There's pump- kins, corn, and to- ma- toes, beans, and car- rots, too.
2. There's one more food stand to vis- it; It's my fav- orite spot.

D.C. al Fine

Ap- ples, squash, and po- ta- toes; All things that the sel- lers grew.
Ris- tras to dec- or- ate with, and grind up to make things hot.

5—Cornhusk Paper

Social Studies, Art, Science

Preparation

Pass around a piece of cornhusk. Ask students how the texture feels. Pass around a soft piece of rag. Have students compare the feel of the rag with that of the cornhusk. Ask the students: If we were to make paper from cornhusks, what texture would you expect? If we were to make paper from rags, what texture would you expect?

In some places in the world, people do make paper from cornhusks. Women in the eastern rainforest of Guatemala make books and bookmarks out of cornhusk paper, which they decorate with cornhusk strips and printed designs.

∅ ∅ ∅

Although making paper from cornhusks is a difficult process, involve students in trying the following simple method for making a cornhusk book or bookmark, which can be decorated with a printed trim.

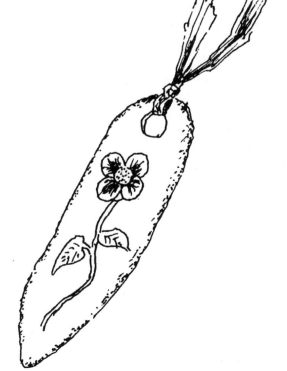

Cornhusk Book and Bookmark

Each Student (or Group) Needs

- Cornhusks
- Felt
- Bucket of water
- Heavy book
- Yarn
- Paper punch
- Scissors

Have Each Student (or Group)

1. Soak cornhusks in water for a few hours.
2. Cut husks into small pages or bookmark-size pieces.
3. Place the cornhusk pages or bookmarks between two pieces of felt, and place a heavy book on top. Leave until dry.
4. Using a paper punch, punch two holes (for a book) along the sides of the pages. Punch one hole at one end for a bookmark.
5. Tie the book together with yarn, or tie a piece of yarn through the hole at the end for a bookmark. Decorate as explained below.

Exploring with Students

How can you make sure the holes on each sheet are in the same places? What can you use to write with on your cornhusk paper?

Extending Ideas

1. Have students make a potato or sponge print with which to decorate their books and bookmarks. Cut a potato in half. On one half, cut a raised design using a plastic knife (etch the design first, and then cut the potato away from the design). Thinly coat the design with tempera paint, and gently print the design on paper. Caution the students to lift the potato from the paper carefully so as not to smear the paint.

   To make a sponge print, cut a sponge into small shapes. Dampen the sponge shapes and squeeze out the excess water. Gently touch the bottom surface of the sponge to the paint. Print the painted surface of the sponge on paper, again being careful not to smear the paint.

Generations of People Who Work with Clay

For generations, people have created objects made from clay. Working with clay is an art form that is passed down through the generations. To bring this idea to life (actual people teaching their children and grandchildren to work with clay), share with students information about Ignacia Duran and her family.

1—Ignacia Duran and Family

Social Studies, Art, Science, Language Arts

Preparation

Clay is a wonderful hands-on material that has been enjoyed by all cultures for generations. Share with students the following account of a potter, Ignacia Duran, as a prelude to the activities that follow.

Ignacia Duran

Ignacia Duran

Ignacia Duran is a Native American potter who lives in Tesuque, New Mexico. She has lived in the pueblo all her life. Ignacia learned how to make pottery from her mother, and she has taught her daughter and her granddaughter how to be potters as well.

Ignacia, her daughter, and her granddaughter make pots and figures from wet clay. They find the clay close to where they live. The finished pieces of pottery are placed in the sun to dry. When each piece is completely dry, it is "fired" in a hot fire outdoors similar to a covered campfire. After the fire has gone out and the clay pieces are cool, they are removed from the ashes. Then they are decorated.

Ignacia's work has a certain style. If you were to see her work mixed with other potters' work, you could probably identify them. This owl is very similar to one she created.

Owl

Ignacia and the people in her pueblo believe that the owl brings a warning. When you see an owl, you should stop and think about what you are doing.

The pottery made by Bea, Ignacia's daughter, looks different from that of her mother. This drawing is of a little jug that Bea created.

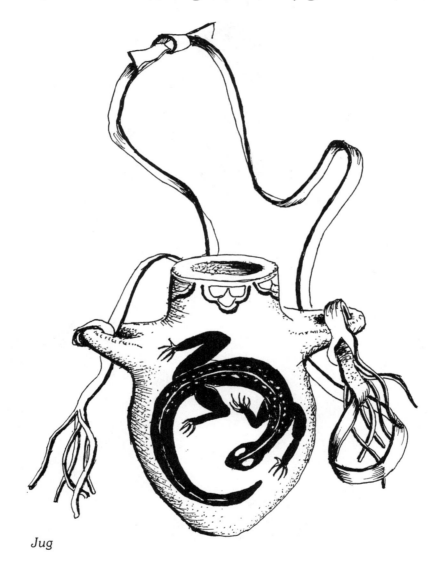

Jug

The strap is made from soft, white buckskin, and the lizard is painted in a soft green color.

The pottery made by Roxanne, Ignacia's granddaughter, also has a unique style. The figures on the next page were drawn from a set Roxanne created.

Kokepelli

The flute player, Kokepelli, is a symbol of harmony. The animals around him represent the harmony of the creatures. Many cultures have a figure similar to Kokepelli.

Activities

1. Have students create a small animal from clay. Have them research the animal's importance in various parts of the world. For example, the quetzal is a popular bird in Central America, and the peacock is the national bird of India. Fire the clay animal and glaze or paint with acrylic or tempera paints.

2. Read to students Rina Swentzell's *Children of Clay: A Family of Pueblo Potters* (1992), a beautiful book about an old potter and her family. It shows them collecting the clay, creating pottery, firing their work, and selling it in their pueblo. Discuss the story with the students.

3. Some Native American children made figures out of clay, and they used the clay figures to tell a story. Involve the students in rolling out a slab of clay and using a plastic knife to cut out several figures. Fire the figures, and have students decorate them. Engage students in telling an oral story, using the figures as characters.

4. The video *Maria* is about Maria Martinez, a famous pueblo potter. It portrays Maria and her son, Popovi Day, as they collect the clay, create and decorate pots, and fire them in a traditional open-pit fire. This video is produced by INTERpark, located at 1540 East MacArthur, Cortez, Colorado 81321. The company can be reached by phone at 970-565-7453.

2—Wedding Vase

Language Arts, Art, Social Studies

Preparation

The wedding vase is a wonderful Native American tradition. It is a beautiful vase usually made by the future husband's parents in anticipation of the wedding and the couple's life together. When the vase is complete, all the relatives go to the bride's home, where the bride displays the items she has collected for her and her future husband's new life. She might show them pots, moccasins, corn, and clothing. Everyone has advice for the new couple, and at this ceremony the married people try to share what they have learned through their lives. The old people want the new couple to be happy, and they share the couple's joy.

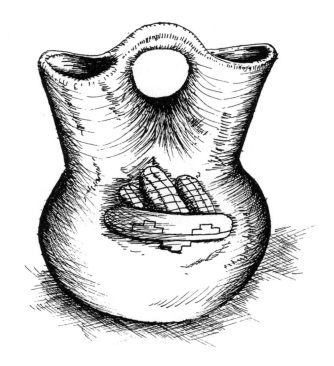

Wedding Vase

In the wedding vase is holy water. The bride drinks from one side of the vase, and she hands the vase to the groom, who drinks from the other side. This ceremony unites the couple as one, and they treasure the vase as long as they both live. When one of them dies, the vase is given to another happily married couple.

Explain to the students that the vases were handmade—meaning that people made them with their hands and not by throwing them on a potter's wheel. They were built using the "coil" and "pinch" methods, as indicated in the activity that follows. Students will enjoy learning these two basic methods of hand building.

∅ ∅ ∅

In the activity that follows, have each student try pinching a small bowl, rolling a coil, and building a small pot. Native American tribes typically created pots using these two methods, which make good introductory art projects for students who do not have much experience working with clay. If students want a challenge, have them continue wrapping coils into two spouts, creating a vessel that resembles the wedding vase.

Each Student Needs

- Potter's clay
- Optional: Found object, such as pine cones or bark, for making textures

Have Each Student

Note: Before beginning, teach students how to roll a coil. A coil is long, thin, and uniform. It should be made by rolling the palms of the hands back and forth over the middle of the coil, working the clay toward the ends of the coil to lengthen it.

1. Roll a small chunk of clay into a ball, about the size of a baseball.
2. Push the thumb into the center of the ball and pinch around the sides using finger and thumb.
3. Roll a coil with additional clay. The coil should be uniform and about ¾ inches in diameter.
4. Wrap the coil around the top rim of the pinched bowl. Roll more coils and lay them one on top of another to build the pot to the desired height.
5. Smooth the coils together, inside or outside the pot, or both.
6. Add texture to the outside of the pot by making impressions using natural materials such as pinecones and bark.
7. When the pots are dry, fire them in a kiln. After firing, paint them with acrylic paints, or glaze them and fire again. If the pots have been painted with acrylic paints, do not fire them again because the paint will burn off at high temperatures.

Exploring with Students

Are you planning a shape for your pot before beginning? Are you keeping the desired shape in mind as you pinch your bowl and wrap the coils to build up the sides? What objects can you use to add texture to your pot?

3—David Gomez's Shop in Mexico

Social Studies, Art, Music, Language Arts

Preparation

Read to students the following story about David Efren Gomez's pottery shop in Mexico as a prelude to the activities that follow.

The Pottery Shop

David Efren Gomez's family has a shop in Tijuana, Mexico. They sell many different types of pottery to tourists and local residents. David tells how some people come every summer to see what new items he and his father have in the shop. David remembers many of his customers and can call them by name even though they may visit the shop only once in a while.

The pottery is made by people in Mexico. In the shop are pots and vases of all sizes, masks, clay necklaces, piñatas, and even clay flutes. If you go into the shop, you will find that the prices are not shown on any of the items. David and his dad will bargain with you. They will tell you a price, and you can ask them to sell it to you for less money. Then they will probably try to raise your price a little higher, and you can name another price if you would like to pay less money. This will continue until you and David are both satisfied with the price.

It is a long day at the shop. On some days, many people come in to bargain, and on other days business is pretty slow. There are other shops in the area that also sell pottery, so David and his dad try to stock their shop with popular and unusual items so the people will buy from them. They are happy when they sell their pottery, and may even throw in a small cornhusk donkey (see p. 95 to create a cornhusk donkey) or a pottery necklace in appreciation for the sale.

David Gomez in His Shop

Activities

1. Have students interview a shopkeeper or owner of a business in which they are interested. What is a day in this shop or business like? Does the shopkeeper or business owner have fixed prices?

2. There are very few places in the United States where shopkeepers will bargain for prices. Often, people having garage sales will bargain. Have students think about the advantages and disadvantages of bargaining with customers. For example, the students might discuss how bargaining may encourage sales but make it difficult to plan profits.

3. "Ten Dollars Is Too Much!" (see pp. 111-12), is a fun and clever song sung between two children or two groups of children. The buyer or buyers sing the parts indicated by the question, and the shopkeeper or shopkeepers respond.

TEN DOLLARS IS TOO MUCH!

Question: Answer:

I'd   like   to   buy   a   hat;   How   much   is   the   price?   My

hats   are   ten   dol-   lars   and   they   are   ve-   ry   nice.

Question: Answer:

Ten   dol-   lars   is   too   much;   Will   you   sell   for   less?   Ten

dol-   lars   is   too   much?   I'll   sell   for   nine   I   guess!
(half   spoken)

("Ten Dollars Is Too Much!" continues on p. 112.)

"Ten Dollars Is Too Much!"—Continued

REPEAT LINES 3 AND 4 USING ONE LESS NUMBER EACH TIME
WHEN YOU REACH "ONE DOLLAR", END WITH THE FOLLOWING:

Question:
One dol- lar is too much; Will you sell for less?

Answer:
You may take the hat! Now, let me have some rest!

4—Open Market in Central America

Social Studies, Art, Language Arts, Music

Preparation

There are few things more colorful than open markets in Central America. Many students may be familiar with farmers markets and how the farmers sell their produce in an open structure. Explain to them that in countries like Guatemala, the majority of the shopping takes place at stands similar to those found at farmers markets. The people bring their bread, fruit, vegetables, meat, and flowers to market and sell them all day. Other merchants bring just about everything one can think of—clothes, shoes, radios, cassette tapes, toys, and household goods, to name a few. The markets are noisy and bustling. Young children help haul water in buckets for the flowers, and others sit with their families at the stands. Young children are strapped on their mothers' backs in pieces of colored material that resemble a shawl.

Share with students the photograph below of a Guatemalan market. Have them compare the photograph with the illustration on p. 114, which shows a miniature clay market stand made by a child. The photograph shows the market in black and white, but one of the most wonderful things about the market stands is how colorful they are. Explain to students that miniature clay market stands are common folk art in Central America. As is true with most cultures, people in Guatemala and other Central American countries create art from their experiences—they make what they know.

Guatemalan Market

In the activity that follows, involve the students in creating a miniature clay market stand. For an interesting variation, have students research markets in other areas of the world and create clay replicas of market stands that sell fabrics, jewelry, and other items.

Clay Market Stand

Each Student Needs

- Paper and pencil
- Potter's clay
- Plastic knife
- Garlic press
- Rolling pin
- Acrylic paints or ceramic stains (bright colors)
- Paintbrushes

Have Each Student

1. Design a flower, fruit, or other market stand on paper. Plan how big it will be and the dimensions of the walls of the stand. If over 6 inches tall or long, the clay will collapse.
2. Roll out slabs of clay to make the floor and walls of the stand. Let them dry for several days until they will hold their shape.
3. Add clay shelves and baskets to the stand.
4. From clay, create the details—people who work in the stand, and the wares that are sold at the stand. Use a garlic press to make thin coils of clay (for flower stems, etc.). Press the wares into the stand.
5. When the stall is dry, fire it in a kiln. Paint the stall, wares, and people with bright colors of ceramic stain or acrylic paint.

Exploring with Students

Can you use a garlic press to make flower stems? What other materials, such as household "junk," can be used to create your market stand?

Extending Ideas

1. Young students will enjoy participating in a drama recreating a Guatemalan market, where they can practice buying and selling different products. Have students pretend to use quetzal bills, the Guatemalan currency. Photocopy and cut out enough currency for the students (see illustration, p. 116). Explain to them that approximately twelve quetzals (½ each) will equal one American dollar. (See also idea 3, below.)

2. The students will be interested in knowing that a quetzal is a colorful, rare bird with very long tail feathers that lives in Central America. The quetzal appears on Guatemalan money. Have students draw a quetzal on a strip of paper about the size of a dollar. Have a color photo of the bird available for the activity.

3. Have students learn a few basic Spanish words for what can be bought at Guatemalan market stands.

English and Spanish Words

flowers = las flores

rose = la rosa

carnation = el clavel

daisy = la margarita

fruits = las frutas

pineapple = la piña

apple = la manzana

mango = el mango

orange = la naranja

banana = el plátano

vegetable = el vegetal

celery = el apio

carrot = la zanahoria

peas = los guisantes

beans = los frijoles

corn = el maíz

please = por favor

thank you = gracias

I would like to buy some . . . = Yo quisiera comprar unos (unas) . . .

How much do these cost? = ¿Cuanto cuestan estos?

If students become confused over the use of the articles, briefly explain to them that some foreign languages designate whether or not the noun is masculine or feminine by the use of specific articles in front of them.

Guatemalan Money

4. Involve the students in making other interesting and fun objects from Central and South America. Have students fashion a chicken with textured feathers, a colorful bus common to the countries, and a sun or moon ornament often seen on adobe houses. (See next activity.)

Chicken: From a small ball of clay, pinch a bowl. Sculpt a head and neck and press it onto the bowl. Place small pinched pieces of clay in rows to resemble feathers. Fire the chicken in a kiln. Leave it as is or paint with tempera or acrylic paints or ceramic stains.

Chicken

Bus: Roll out a slab of clay with a rolling pin. Using a plastic knife, cut the sides, bottom, and top of a bus. Join the clay pieces at the seams. Add clay baskets and other items on top of the bus. Fire the bus in a kiln and paint with bright colors of tempera paint, acrylic paint, or ceramic stains.

Bus

5—Clay Moon and Sun

Social Studies, Art, Science, Language Arts

Preparation

People everywhere share the experience of the sun and moon. In all cultures, across all lands, people have thought about the moon and sun and their mysteries. Ask the students what they know about the sun and the moon. Write their ideas on a large chart, and discuss their comments. Also include questions they might have.

Stories about the sun and moon have been told through the generations, in every part of the world. Storytellers told these stories in an effort to understand the sun and moon and to express their thoughts about what they saw happening in the sky in relation to their lives—they depended on sunlight for crops, they played in the sun, and they watched the cycles of the moon.

Legends of the Sun and Moon (1983) by Eric Hadley and Tessa Hadley is an excellent collection of stories that try to explain the sun and moon. The legends are Aboriginal, Nigerian, Armenian, Polynesian, West African, Haitian, and Native American. Read and explore some of these legends with the students, or tell stories from other resources.

Clay moons and suns are popular folk art objects because of the timeless interest in astronomy and astrology.

✆ ✆ ✆

In the activity that follows, involve the students in creating a clay moon or sun of their own.

Each Student Needs

- Potter's clay or baker's dough
    To make baker's dough, mix and chill: 4 cups flour, 1 cup salt, and 1½ cups water.
- Plastic knife
- Rolling pin
- Tempera paints, acrylic paints, or ceramic stains
- Paintbrushes
- Optional: Cookie sheet if using baker's dough and oven

Have Each Student

Sun

1. Roll a slab of clay with a rolling pin (about ¼ inch thick).
2. Using a plastic knife, cut out a circle for the center, and cut out small rectangular or teardrop shapes for the rays.
3. Attach the rays to the center. Pinch or carve a face into the surface of the sun.
4. Fire the clay sun in a kiln, and paint with tempera paints, acrylic paints, or ceramic stains. If baker's dough is used, bake in a 350° F oven for 1½ hours.

Sun

Moon

1. Roll a slab of clay with a rolling pin (about ¼ inch thick).
2. Using a plastic knife, cut out a crescent shape resembling a portion of the moon.
3. Pinch or carve a face into the surface of the moon.
4. Fire the clay moon in a kiln, and paint with tempera or acrylic paints, or ceramic stains. If baker's dough is used, bake in a 350° F oven for 1½ hours.

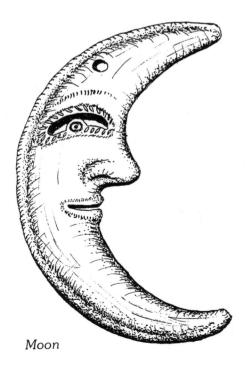

Moon

Exploring with Students

Can you use your finger to make the surface of the sun or moon smooth, or would you rather have a different texture for the surface? What do you know about the sun? The moon?

Extending Ideas

1. Have students chart the phases of the moon for one month, drawing a picture of the moon each night to observe the moon's cycles.

6—African Necklace

Social Studies, Art

Preparation

Have a photograph of an Akua-ba doll for the children to look at. Explain that Akua-ba dolls are made by African women in Ghana. The doll is worn tucked in the woman's waistband or around her neck as a symbol of future healthy children. The woman wears a square-headed doll if she wants a girl or a round-headed doll if she wants a boy. (For more information, see *The Art of Africa* [1965] by Shirley Glubok.)

℘ ℘ ℘

In the activity that follows, involve the students in making a doll necklace.

Each Student Needs

- Potter's clay or baker's dough
  To make baker's dough, mix and chill: 4 cups flour, 1 cup salt, and 1½ cups water.
- Plastic knife
- Rolling pin
- Pencil
- Acrylic or tempera paints, or ceramic stains
- Paintbrushes
- Yarn
- Scissors

Have Each Student

1. Roll out slab of clay between ⅛- to ¼-inch thick.
2. Lightly sketch a doll figure on the clay with a pencil.
3. Cut out the doll with a plastic knife.
4. If using potter's clay, smooth the edges of the doll with a finger.
5. Using a pencil, poke a hole at the top of the doll.
6. If using potter's clay, fire the doll in a kiln. If using baker's dough, air dry or bake in an oven at 350° F for 1½ hours.
7. Paint the doll using acrylic or tempera paints, or ceramic stains.
8. String with a piece of yarn.

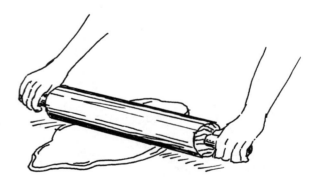

Making an African Necklace

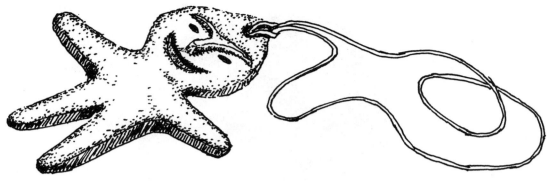

African Necklace

Exploring with Students

Are you rolling out the clay so that it is between ⅛- to ¼-inch thick? What colors would you paint your doll if you wanted it to look similar to one made in Africa?

7—Masks

Social Studies, Art

Preparation

Masks are worn by people all over the world during ceremonies, plays, parades, dances, and even at certain funerals (in Asia). Masks are also worn for protection, to worship ancestors, to act out stories, and when performing healing ceremonies. Have several books about masks from various parts of the world available for the students to examine.

∅ ∅ ∅

In the activity that follows, involve the students in creating miniature masks similar to those that most intrigue them. Challenge the students to design original masks, but they must be prepared to explain which types of masks influenced their creation. In Africa, miniature versions of traditional masks are made into necklaces. A student may want to punch a hole at the top of the mask and make a necklace.

Each Student Needs
- Potter's clay
- Feathers
- Glue
- Paints
- Paintbrushes
- String or yarn
- Decorative materials (feathers, fabric, bric-a-brac, small buttons, etc.)

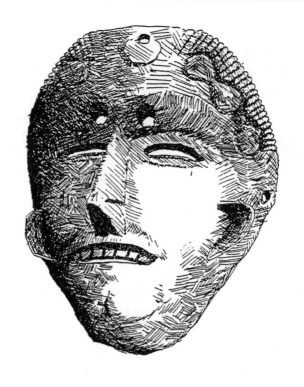

Masks

Have Each Student

1. Roll the clay into a ball the size of a small fist. Flatten the ball with the palm of the hand.

2. Pinch a face into the clay.

3. Poke a hole at the top of the mask if it will be made into a necklace.

4. Fire the face in a kiln.

5. Decorate the mask using feathers, fabric, small buttons, paint, and other decorative materials.

6. Share the mask with a classmate. Tell who would have worn the mask and when they might have worn it.

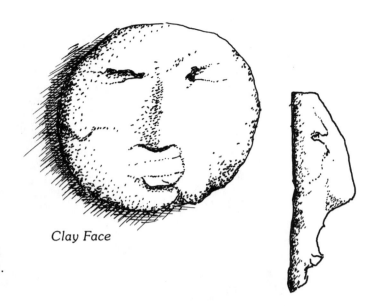

Clay Face

Exploring with Students

Would it be helpful to design your mask on paper before creating it with clay? What are you adding to your mask to make it unique?

8—Mamie Deschillie

Social Studies, Art

Preparation

Mamie Deschillie is a Navajo folk artist. She is famous for her "mud toys" and her "cardboards." Mamie learned to make the mud toys when she was a child. She mixed clay with water, formed the figures, baked them in the sun, and decorated them with paints, cloth, paper, and many other materials. When she was older, she began cutting shapes out of heavy cardboard and decorating them. She is the first Navajo artist to try such an unusual art form. The cutouts are of various sizes. Some are five feet tall!

Mamie's artwork is in museums and other public and private collections. She is truly a creative artist. From clay, Mamie sculpts zebras with chickens riding on their backs and sheep with wooly coats. Her cardboard cutouts include a Santa Claus dressed in a red suit, which is made from a pair of old, red underwear. One cutout and mud toy is a Navajo man or woman riding a horse. The horse is an important symbol in Navajo life and tradition. In Navajo mythology, Sun Bearer created horses by having the Spirit People breathe life into pieces of turquoise, abalone, and shells. His son had two heaps of soil that were turned into a donkey and a horse from the Spirit People's breath.

Mamie is featured in the book *The People Speak: Navajo Folk Art* (1994) by Chuck Rosenak and Jan Rosenak.

∅ ∅ ∅

If possible, show the students a photograph of one of Mamie's mud toys or cardboard cutouts, or share with them one you may have created ahead of time. Then involve them in creating a mud toy or cardboard cutout of their own.

Mamie Deschillie Mud Toys

Clay Toy

Each Student Needs

- Clay or baker's dough
  To make baker's dough, mix and chill: 4 cups flour, 1 cup salt, and 1½ cups water.
- Fabrics, wool, and other decorative materials
- Paints: tempera or acrylic
- Paintbrushes
- Glue

Have Each Student

1. Create a toy from clay.
2. Place it in the sun (outside or on a plate in a window).
3. When dry, paint the toy.
4. Glue on wool, fabric, and other decorative materials as desired.

Exploring with Students

How are you deciding what to sculpt out of your clay? What did you learn through the process of sculpting your toy? Did you add natural materials to decorate your toy, or were they humanmade?

Cardboard Cutouts

Each Student Needs

- Large pieces of cardboard or tagboard (tagboard is easier to cut)
- Fabrics and other decorative materials
- Markers, tempera paints, and bric-a-brac
- Paintbrushes
- Glue
- Scissors

Have Each Student

1. Cut out a cardboard figure of a person or animal (an adult may have to help).
2. Using markers, paints, and bric-a-brac, create details, such as eyes and a mouth.
3. Glue on fabrics and other decorative materials.

Exploring with Students

Are you making an image of yourself? Does your figure look true to life, or is it whimsical, like Mamie's chicken riding on a zebra?

Extending Ideas

1. Read to students the book *The Mud Pony* (1988) by Caron Lee Cohen. In this story, a boy makes a pony out of mud, but unlike Mamie Deschillie's horses that sit on the shelf, this horse came to life!
2. Several years ago in Colorado, a cardboard doll project began. The Colorado Children's Campaign began this project in an effort to make Colorado a better place for children. The cardboard dolls are made by children, senior groups, prison inmates, and others, then taken to business offices to remind people to be advocates for children. Talk with students about this idea—cardboard children used as symbols for children. The National Association for the Education of Young Children has designated one week each spring as the Week of the Young Child. Have students create and hang cardboard cutouts of themselves during this week.

Navajo Weaving

1—A Herder's Goat

Social Studies, Art, Language Arts

Preparation

On the Navajo reservation, many families have long-haired goats like the ones in the photograph below. It is fun to watch them wandering along the edge of a dirt road, by a hogan, or through the brush. From this photograph, the students will be able to tell that the goat provides a lot of hair when it is shorn!

Long-Haired Goats

Some families raise goats for their milk, hair, and meat, and others have goats for pets. Share with students books about goats: In the book *Navajo Pet* (1971) by Patricia Miles Martin, a Navajo boy has a goat who is very good friends with his friend's horse. *The Goat in the Rug* (1990) by Charles L. Blood and Martin A. Link is a delightful book about a long-haired goat whose wool coat is woven into a Navajo rug. (If you share this book with students, be sure to point out that most hogans do not look like the one pictured, but have six sides.) Ann Nolan Clark's *Little Herder in Autumn* (1988) is a lovely book written in Navajo and English.

Folk art goats are made from wood and goat hair and are sold at some trading posts on the Navajo reservation.

∅ ∅ ∅

In the activity that follows, have students make a similar goat using a block of foam and artificial materials for the hair.

Each Student Needs
- 3-by-3-by-5-inch block of foam
- Scissors
- Four wood dowels, ½-inch in diameter by 3-inches long
- Glue
- White tempera paint
- Paintbrush
- Beige or off-white artificial fur, or dyed wool (available at craft stores)
- Small black piece of felt or paper, or black paint or marker
- Two toothpicks

Have Each Student
1. Round one end of the block of foam to make the goat's head.
2. Paint the head white. Add black eyes with paper, felt, paint, or marker.
3. Make four holes in the block of foam to hold the legs.
4. Glue dowels into the holes.
5. Cut the artificial fur or dyed wool into strips and pieces, and glue it around the block of foam.
6. Insert toothpicks for horns.

Exploring with Students
What do you know about the habits of goats? In the famous song "Bill Grogan's Goat," the goat eats clothing right off the clothesline. Can goats really eat something "right off the line"?

Goat

Extending Ideas

1. In Peru, people make a similar folk toy, but it is a llama instead of a goat. Llamas are commonly used to carry people and their wares from location to location. Have students make llamas with blocks of foam, dowels, and wool, and decorate them with colorful pompons and tiny pinched clay pots. (See p. 108 on pinching pots.)

   What would you want to ask someone who has made a trip through the Andes on a llama? Would riding a llama be like riding a horse?

Llama

2—Old Ways, New Ways

Social Studies, Art, Language Arts, Science

Preparation

Read to students "Old Ways, New Ways," a short story written by fourth-grade student Rosalie Thompson, as a prelude to the activities that follow.

Old Ways, New Ways

Once, my grandpa told me a story. It all got started because we had gone to help shear the sheep. The men shearing the sheep filled huge burlap bags with wool to the very top. They had the bag jumper, who stood inside the bag, and as wool was being tossed up, he put it in the bag and jumped on it to push it down as far as it would go.

The men rolled the fleece up and tied it with twine. I tried to pick up a bundle and toss it up to the bag jumper, but it was way too heavy because it weighed about 30 pounds. The wool felt greasy and tough, and when I tried to pull it apart, it was very stringy like all sorts of spider webs put together.

When they were all done shearing the sheep, I asked my grandfather if I could take a little bit of wool home. He said that would be just fine. He asked me what I was going to do with it. I told him I was going to make a pouch. He asked me, "Why don't you make a rug like they did in the tribe?" I asked him what he was talking about, and he said, "Our tribe."

I hadn't heard much about the tribe, but I really listened as he told me how they sheared the sheep when he was a boy and brought the wool into the hogans. He remembered his sister sitting by the big loom outside the hogan, weaving with their mother. He remembered hearing his mother telling his other, little sister to go fetch the berries and flowers to dye the wool. He and his brothers helped crush the flowers and berries. His grandmother boiled them to make the dye. He told me that most girls today do not like to weave rugs like that because they take too much time and too much patience.

After we were done watching them shear the sheep and talking to my grandfather, I took the wool home. I boiled the wool to take out the dirt and greasy feeling from the lanolin. Then I carded the wool. I didn't dye it the old way with berries and flowers, but instead I dyed it with clothing dye. I dyed it in shades of red, grey, blue, purple, and green. I dyed it by putting dye in the jar with water and adding a clump of wool about as big as my fist.

After a while, I took the wool out and laid it on top of the heater. Then I was ready to spin the wool into yarn that I could weave. Since I was just weaving a little thing, I could roll it on my leg to spin it. I had made a cardboard loom, and I started to weave my bag. I thought about what kind of design I wanted to make. My grandpa suggested a design like his sister used to make. He showed me a rug his mother had made for him. He told me that the design on this rug was bisymmetrical. I asked him what bisymmetrical meant. He explained, "If you cut a rug into four pieces, each one would look exactly the same." He pointed to the little line that led out of the rug. He told me that it was there to let the spirits out.

When I was done weaving the bag, I made a handle and hung the bag on the wall. My grandpa said they didn't used to make handles. He liked my handle and told me it was nice. I smiled at him and he smiled back. It felt good that I could weave like the rest of my family.

Rosy's Illustration (the fourth-grade child who wrote the preceding story)

Loom

Activities

1. Have students use yarn to weave a small bag. Make a cardboard loom from a 6-by-4-inch piece of cardboard. Starting ⅛ inch from the edge, cut ¼-inch slits, ¼ inch apart, along each 6-inch edge. Wrap the loom with yarn: Begin at slit A (tie a knot so the yarn does not slip through). Bring the yarn up through slit A, wrap it around the cardboard through slit B and back up through slit A. Cross over the cardboard to slit C, go down through slit C, around the cardboard through slit D and back down through slit C. Cross under to slit E, and repeat as you started at slit A. Repeat until the loom is completely threaded. (See illustrations.)

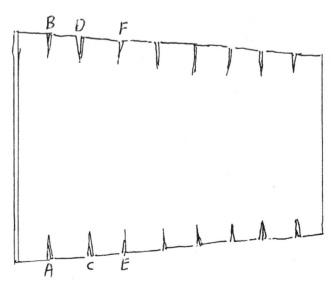

Cardboard Loom

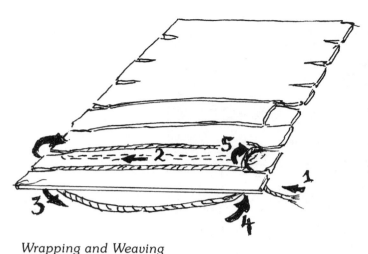

Wrapping and Weaving

To weave, begin at the bottom corner and weave a piece of yarn (about one yard long) under, over, under, over, and so on across the side. When you come to the edge, flip the loom over and continue weaving on the other side, then flip again. As you complete each row, push the yarn toward the bottom. When the weaving is complete (to the top of the loom), cut the top tabs off the loom with small scissors and slip it out from inside the woven bag. Using a yarn needle, sew together the bottom of the bag. Make a small handle by braiding three pieces of yarn. Attach the yarn cord to the bag by tying one end of the cord to each upper corner of the bag.

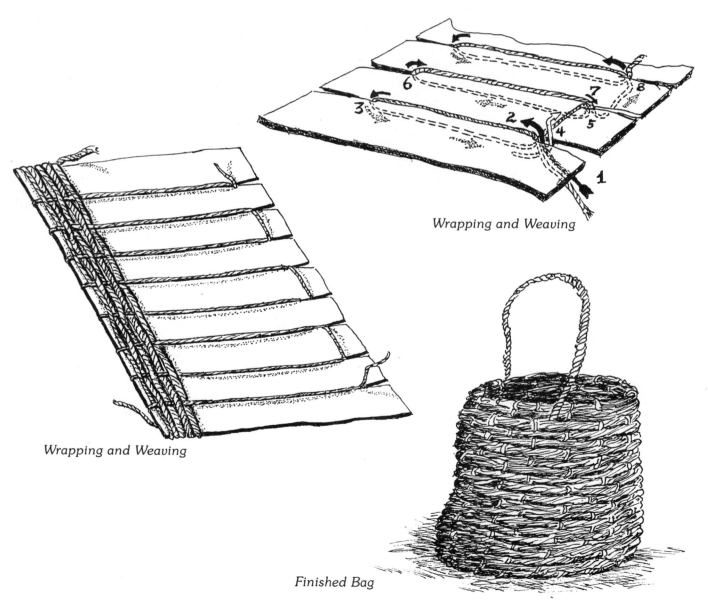

Wrapping and Weaving

Wrapping and Weaving

Finished Bag

3—Designing a Navajo Rug

Social Studies, Art

Preparation

Navajo rugs are woven by Navajo women and are beautiful in design, color, and workmanship. They are all-wool, which traditionally came from the sheep they owned. The weaver has a design in her head—it is not written down. No two rugs are exactly alike. Navajo women on different parts of the reservation produce rugs of distinctive style, pattern, and color.

Ø Ø Ø

Navajo Rug

In the activity that follows, have students use paper to design a Navajo rug. Traditional patterns include geometric designs; a storm pattern depicting the four points of the compass, two waterbugs, lightning, and two whirlwinds; wavy, parallel lines; and ceremonial dancers.

Each Student Needs
- ¼-by-¼-inch graph paper
- Red, black, yellow, brown, and beige markers
- Yarn
- Hole punch

Paper Rug

Have Each Student

1. Design a pattern.
2. Color with a marker.
3. Punch a hole in each corner.
4. Tie a yarn tassel in each hole.

Exploring with Students

What colors are you using in your design? Are they colors the Navajo may have used when weaving?

Variation

Have students try designing a rug from another country. How might the weaving pattern differ from that of a Navajo rug?

Extending Ideas

1. Share with students *Annie and the Old One* (1990) by Miska Miles, a moving and beautiful story of a young Native American girl coming to terms with life, death, and family traditions.

Gourds

1—Decorative Gourds

Social Studies, Science, Art, Language Arts

Preparation

Traditionally, dried gourds have been used around the world for bowls, canteens, baskets, jars, mugs, toys, musical instruments, and even bird houses. The students will enjoy the process of drying a gourd and then creating an object.

Have several varieties of gourds available for the students to examine. How do the gourds feel? Explain to the students that they will set the gourds in a sunny window. Ask the students what might happen to the gourd over a period of time. Record their predictions on a large chart.

The gourds will take a long time to dry—allow several weeks. Because a hollow gourd will dry more quickly, help students safely cut the gourds in half using a handsaw. Have them remove the "meat." When the gourds are dry, involve the students in examining them. How are the gourds different from students' predictions? Guide the students in comparing what actually happened to their predictions

℘ ℘ ℘

In the activity that follows, involve the students in decorating gourds with decorations similar to those used in different parts of the world.

Each Student Needs
- Gourd

Depending on the technique:
- Nail or linoleum knife
- Watercolors, lacquer paints, acrylic paints
- Paintbrushes
- Hot wax (refer to the Batik section)

Have Each Student

1. Review safety precautions for using sharp instruments.
2. Help students cut a gourd in half using a handsaw. Cut the gourd before it has dried and clean out the pulp. If a whole, dried gourd is to be painted, it does not need to be cut in half.
3. Decorate the gourd using one of the following techniques:

Watercolor Design—Guatemala

Paint a design on the sides of a dried gourd using acrylic or watercolor paints.

Guatemalan Gourd

Wax Resist—Peru

Brush hot wax in a design on the side of a dried gourd. When the wax is dry, paint over the waxed surface to create a patterned design (the wax will resist the paint). Leave the wax on the gourd (wax is usually burned or melted off—but that is not recommended for children).

Peruvian Gourd

Carved and Painted—Other Areas of South America and Various Areas of Africa

Cover the surface of a fresh, whole gourd with lacquer or acrylic paint. Using a nail or linoleum knife, carve out a design on the surface of the gourd.

South American/African Gourd

Painted—China and Japan

Paint a dried gourd to resemble an animal, incorporating the entire gourd into the design (black acrylic or lacquer paint works well).

Chinese Gourds

Exploring with Students

How long did it take the gourds to dry? How are you deciding which techniques to use on your gourd? What type of design are you planning? Can you paint the inside of the gourd as well as the outside?

Colorful Cloth

Printing Cloth

1—Object Printing

Art, Social Studies, Language Arts, Music

Preparation

Have various pieces of printed fabric available for the students to feel and examine. Tell them that printing cloth is a very old art of East India and has been practiced (like batik and tie-dyeing) in many countries, such as Africa, where the adrinka fabric is made by the Ashanti people of Ghana. The adrinka cloth is stamped with designs carved from gourds, but fabric can be printed with numerous objects to create various patterns and designs.

Printing cloth is an adventure. Students can make prints using sponges, potatoes, odds and ends, natural materials, and even old bicycle tires! Have the students watch as you dip the flat edge of a sponge into paint and then press the sponge onto a sheet of paper to make a print. Encourage the students to brainstorm about what objects would make a good print.

✄   ✄   ✄

In the activity that follows, involve students in experimenting with various objects, colors, and designs to create cloth that is interesting, creative, and colorful.

Each Student Needs
- Objects to print with
- Acrylic paints
- Fabric
- Paintbrushes
- Shallow dish or pan for paint

Have Each Student

1. Dip or roll the object in the paint, or brush the paint onto the object's surface.
2. Print a pattern on fabric.
3. Try several objects to create a design, or use the same object in a repetitive pattern.
4. Trade prints with a classmate and guess which objects made which prints.

Tire/Hand Print on Fabric

Exploring with Students

Which objects in the environment would make interesting prints? Are you creating a pattern by combining impressions of different objects? By combining colors? Which colors look attractive together?

Extending Ideas

1. Have students make prints on a T-shirt. Set the design into the fabric by ironing the back of the shirt after it is printed. Use a paper bag or newspaper as backing.
2. Arrange a class field trip to a printing shop to watch how newspapers and book pages are printed. After the field trip, record on a large chart the experience and what was learned. Illustrate the printing processes.
3. Share with students the technique of Mayan Printing: This printing technique is used in Central America. A block of wood is carved with a design or symbol. Fabric is placed over the block. A soft cloth mallet is dipped into paint or ink on a dish and hit onto the fabric repeatedly, in quick, brisk strokes. The design or symbol is thereby "stamped" onto the fabric, making an attractive print to share with others.

4. Ask students: What patterns do you see in the world around you? Engage students in thinking about the various patterns they observe each day—on wallpaper, in clouds, on the soles of their shoes, and so on. Discuss with students the patterns they hear each day, such as a baby's cry or the chirping of birds. Involve students in singing the song "Patterns," p. 144.

T-shirt with Leaf Prints

PATTERNS

Pat- terns, pat- terns, eve- ry- where, pat- terns all a- round;

Fine

Pat- terns you can see and touch and e- ven hear in sound.

1. There are
2. There are
3. There are

pat- terns on the clothes you wear and in the stars at night; There are
pat- terns on the soles of shoes and on the walls and floors; There are
pat- terns in a for- est green and in a cloud- y sky; There are

D.C. al Fine

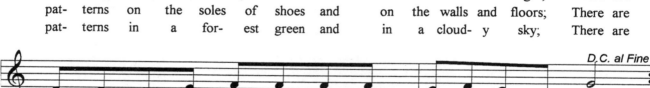

pat- terns in a tele- phone's ring and in a rain- bow bright.
pat- terns in a clock's "tick tock" and on the o- cean's shores.
pat- terns on your favo- rite chair and in a ba- by's cry.

2—Monoprinting

Social Studies, Art, Science

Preparation

Have students fingerpaint on paper. After they wash their hands but while the paint is still wet on the paper, have them carefully lay a clean sheet of paper onto the painting. Have students apply pressure to the paper using a rolling pin, then carefully peel the top paper from the bottom paper. Explain to them that this process of "picking up" a design from a flat surface is called monoprinting.

Demonstrate making a monoprint by painting a design on a piece of glass or plastic, or by coating the entire surface of the glass or plastic with paint and then scratching a design into the paint using a comb, a stick, your finger, and so on. While the paint is still wet, place fabric on the glass or plastic (have a student help). Carefully lift the fabric from the painted surface. Place another piece of scrap material on the painted surface (do not apply more paint). Ask students: What will the design on this second piece of fabric look like? Explain to the students that monoprints are unique because it is difficult to make more than one print from the design, and no two prints are identical. That is why it is called *mono*printing.

∅ ∅ ∅

In the activity that follows, involve students in making a monoprint of their own.

Each Student Needs

- Fabric paint
- Paintbrush
- Tools to make designs (comb, sponge, fork, etc.)
- 8-by-10-inch sheet of glass (size can vary, depending on the size of material to be colored)
- Square of fabric (the size of glass or plastic)

Have Each Student

1. Paint a design on the glass or plastic (or paint the entire surface and scratch a design using a variety of tools).
2. With a classmate, carefully set the fabric on the glass or plastic. Slowly peel the fabric from the glass or plastic.
3. Lay the fabric on a flat surface to dry. (See illustration, p. 146.)

Exploring with Students

What objects can you find that make unusual designs in the paint? Are you painting a design, or scratching one into the paint? Will the colors you have selected look good with the color of the fabric?

Extending Ideas

1. Have students place natural materials such as flowers and grasses on the painted glass or plastic. When the fabric is peeled away, the design will include interesting outlines of the natural materials.

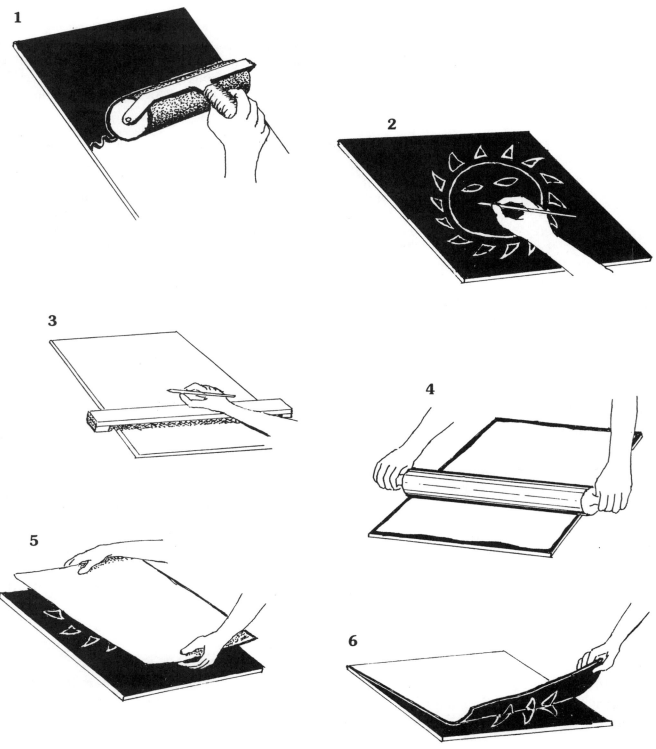

Steps for Monoprinting

Stitching on Cloth

1—Buttons

Social Studies, Science, Art, Language Arts

Preparation

Have a wide assortment of buttons available for students to examine. Ask the students to group the buttons by category. Some students will group by size, some by color, some by shape, and so on. Some students might group the buttons according to use—for example, they might group plain buttons used for fastening clothing separately from decorative buttons used for decorating clothing. Explain that these are a few of the many ways of classifying objects. Which button is their favorite? Ask students to arrange the buttons in a pattern, and discuss the criteria they used to create the pattern.

As a class, brainstorm a list of items that have buttons. Tell students that they will be decorating a fabric item with buttons, and they will need to carefully examine and group buttons as they plan their designs.

Before beginning the activity that follows, demonstrate for students how to safely sew a button onto fabric.

Each Student Needs
- Fabric item to decorate (backpack, baseball cap, tennis shoes, etc.)
- Thread and needle
- Variety of buttons (large quantities are sometimes available at garage sales)

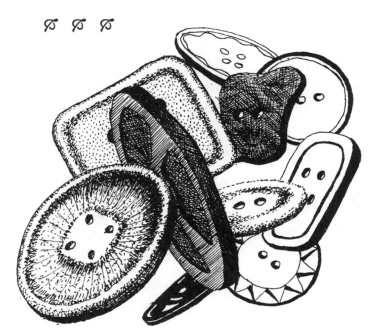

Buttons

Have Each Student

1. Bring to class a fabric item to decorate.
2. Plan a design and select the buttons.
3. Sew the buttons onto the fabric.

Exploring with Students

What are the shapes, sizes, and colors of your buttons? How can you keep a button in place as you sew it onto the fabric?

Variation: Button Blankets

1. Have shells available for the students to examine (and buttons made from shells, if available). Explain to students that some people make buttons from shells because shells are readily available in the environment. Tribal Native Americans on the Northwest Coast make button blankets to wear during ceremonies. Members of each clan sew onto their blankets the image of a special animal (bear, eagle, deer, beaver, salmon, otter, owl) that is a symbol for the clan. They decorate the image with buttons made from shells.

   Have each student cut out a felt or paper animal (black or brown felt or construction paper). Help the students glue or sew their animals onto a large piece of earth-colored fabric or paper. Have each student glue or sew buttons onto the figures to create a class mural.

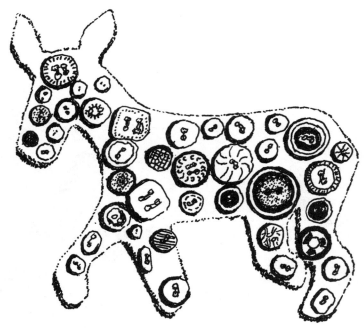

Button Donkey

Extending Ideas

1. Involve the students in singing the song "Patterns" (see p. 144).
2. Have the students read Phillis Gershator's *Tukama Tootles the Flute: A Tale from the Antilles* (1994) and *Love Flute* (1992) by Paul Goble, both interesting books about sound patterns.

2—Arpilleras (Ar-pee-YAIR-ahs)— Peruvian Wall Hangings

Social Studies, Art, Language Arts

Preparation

Arpilleras are brightly colored wall hangings created by the women and men in Peru. Read to students the book *Tonight Is Carnaval* (1991) by Arthur Dorros, a story about a family in South America who is excitedly preparing for Carnival (*Carnaval* in Spanish). The book is illustrated with arpilleras. It concludes with an explanation and depiction of how men and women in Peru create the wall hangings.

Talk with the students about how the wall hangings are made from colorful pieces of fabric, which are cut and placed on a large fabric background. Each shape is neatly stitched around its outer edge with embroidery floss. Three-dimensional objects such as dolls, baskets, fruits, and vegetables are added. Often, people will work together as they sew. Point out that there are quilting groups in many of our communities, and that a Peruvian wall hanging is similar to a quilt in that for both, pieces of fabric are sewn together.

Lead the students in thinking and talking about the scene in a Peruvian wall hanging, such as one in the book *Tonight Is Carnaval*. The scenes on arpilleras represent life in Peru. Guide the students in looking at the llamas and fields. Explain that many Peruvian villages are agricultural. In Peru, llamas are used as pack animals, and their wool is used in weaving.

✁ ✁ ✁

In the activity that follows, involve the students in creating a group or individual arpillera, Peruvian-style. A colorful Peruvian-style hanging can be created using fabrics or construction paper.

Each Student (or Group) Needs

- Fabric or construction paper
- Glue
- Scissors
- Large, white piece of fabric or construction paper
- Fine-tipped black marker
- Optional: Nylon hose for heads and fabric scraps for bodies

Have Each Student (or Group)

1. Think of a scene for a Peruvian-style wall hanging.
2. Cut out pieces of fabric or construction paper to make the scene.
3. Glue the fabric or construction paper pieces onto the larger piece of fabric or construction paper.

4. With a fine-tipped black marker, make small lines around each shape to represent stitches.

5. Make small likenesses of people and other three-dimensional objects such as buildings, animals, and plants and glue them on the wall hanging.

6. Write a poem or a story about the scene. Hang the wall hanging and the writing together on the wall.

Peruvian Wall Hanging

Exploring with Students

Are you creating a scene that would be found in Peru, or is the scene a representation of something *you* have experienced? If it is something you have experienced, does it still look like a Peruvian hanging? Why? Appliqué (just below) is another process that can be used to create wall hangings.

3—Appliqué

Social Studies, Art

Preparation

Similar to arpilleras, appliqués are an art form in other areas of the world. For example, in Africa, appliqués were used for flags and wall hangings that told stories of specific kingdoms. The word *appliqué* is French, meaning "to add or apply." These colorful pieces of cloth were often used for wall decorations or clothing in ancient Egypt, India, and Europe.

Show students the illustration (see p. 152) and ask them what they notice about it. Call their attention to the fact that the figures have been stitched to the background. Show the students a photograph or piece of fabric that has been appliquéd. Ask students to think about where they have seen appliquéd fabric. They may have seen a quilt or a backpack with appliquéd designs.

✄ ✄ ✄

In the activity that follows, involve the students in creating an appliqué of their own.

Each Student Needs

- Scraps of various fabrics and a large piece for the background
- Scissors
- Pins
- Thread and needle
- Paper and pencil
- Optional: Tea (before the activity, soak white fabric in tea to give it an off-white, old appearance)
- Buttons, beads, feathers, bric-a-brac, and other decorative materials

Have Each Student

1. Plan images for the appliqué and draw them on a sheet of paper.
2. Select a fabric for the background and place it aside temporarily. Earth-tone colors work well, or plain white or beige fabric can be dyed with tea.
3. Cut out the images from the paper pattern and pin them onto various scraps on fabrics. Cut out fabric images, leaving a ¼-inch border around each image (this edge will be turned under when the image is sewn onto the background).

4. Cut thin strips of fabric (2 inches wide) to form a border around the background.

5. Sew the border to the background, with the front sides of the fabric facing together.

6. Turn under the edges of the images and sew them to the background (using a straight stitch).

7. Sew on buttons, beads, feathers, bric-a-brac, or other decorative materials as desired.

Appliqué

Exploring with Students

Why are you selecting these particular fabrics? Do the patterns and colors complement the images in your appliqué?

4—Stories in Burlap

Art, Language Arts, Social Studies, Science

Preparation

Stories told from one generation to another can be captured with stitchery on burlap. The story can be one of historical significance, such as the battle at Gettysburg, or one that has been told in a family for many years. Brainstorm with the students about stories they would like to bring alive on a piece of burlap.

Story on Burlap

Demonstrate a few basic stitching techniques for the students. Have students practice the stitches with you on squares of burlap. (See stitch samples below.)

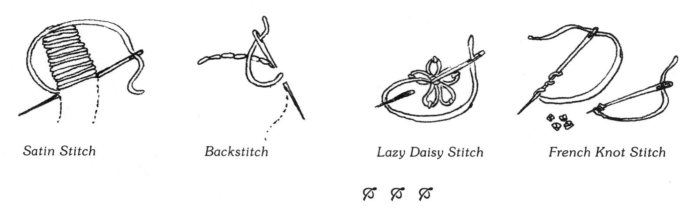

Satin Stitch   Backstitch   Lazy Daisy Stitch   French Knot Stitch

☍ ☍ ☍

In the activity that follows, involve the students in creating a visual story of their own.

Each Student Needs

- Paper and pencil
- Yarn
- Yarn needle
  Note: Talk with children about handling the needle carefully. Plastic yarn needles may be best for younger children.
- Piece of burlap (available by the yard at fabric stores)
- Scissors

Have Each Student

1. Sketch the visual story on paper.
2. Use several basic stitches to create the story using yarn on a piece of burlap.
3. Share the burlap stitchery with a classmate and tell its story.

Exploring with Students

What can you do to keep the edges of the burlap from raveling? Can you stitch them under or cover the edges with tape? Are you using a variety of stitches on your picture, or are you creating the entire stitchery with one or two stitches?

Extending Ideas

1. Have students make a stitchery map rather than a visual story. Explore different types of maps with the students (a child's room, a constellation, the route of a historical journey, a scene from a book, etc.). Show the students the key on a sample map, and talk about the various symbols included in keys so people can find things on a map. Have students include a key on their stitchery map, made from paper and stitched or taped on the map, or stitched into the burlap.

2. Creating and stitching designs on burlap makes for a wonderful free-time activity. Have students keep a square of burlap in their desk or tote tray for stitching fields of flowers, stripes, trees, or anything of interest. Have students write a poem to accompany their stitchery.

Dyeing Fabric

1—Batiking

Art, Social Studies, Science

Preparation

Batiking was originally done by people on the island of Java, and later was adopted by many countries throughout the world. Batiking is the process of painting wax on fabric and then dipping the fabric into, or painting it with, dye.

Batiking

Demonstrate the batiking process for the students. Have students watch as you color with crayon on a piece of paper. Paint over the crayon using watercolors. What happens? Explain to the students that the wax resists the paint, and that this is the basis for the traditional way of decorating cloth using a wax resist—batik.

∅ ∅ ∅

155

In the activity that follows, involve students in trying this wax resist technique themselves.

Each Student (or Group) Needs

- Fabric dye, one or two colors (prepared according to package directions)
- Water
- Paraffin (beeswax can be used but is more expensive)
- Paintbrushes
- White cotton or silk fabric
- Coffee can or pan
- Large pan with water
- Hot plate or stove burner
- Optional: A batik pot (or crockpot) can also be used instead of the above three items.
- Newspapers
- Iron
- Paper bag or newspaper
- Pencil
- Cooking thermometer

Have Each Student (or Group)

1. Plan a design, and draw it with pencil on fabric.
2. Place the paraffin, beeswax, or combination of the two into a coffee can or pan. To melt it, place the coffee can in a pan of hot water on a hot plate or stove burner.

> Safety Note: Have only a few students (or one group) at a time melt wax. Supervise students as they melt the wax. (As an alternative, use crayons instead of hot wax— see "Variation: Crayon Wax Resist," below.) Do not touch the pan, water, hotplate, or melted wax with your hands. If the wax begins to smoke, immediately unplug the hotplate or turn off the stove.

3. Paint the wax onto the fabric following the design. It will harden almost immediately.
4. Paint over the cloth with one color of dye.
5. When the dye is dry, rinse the fabric in cold water.
6. Hang the fabric to dry.

Steps 1–3, Batiking

7. To remove the wax: Place a paper bag or newspaper on an ironing board or a table. Place the fabric on the newspaper and another newspaper on top of the fabric. Iron over the paper; the newspaper will absorb the wax. Replace the paper when it becomes saturated with wax. Iron the fabric several times, until the wax has been completely absorbed.

8. Add a second color of dye, if desired, by repeating the process.

Step 7, Batiking

Exploring with Students

What are you learning about dyes? How is painting with wax like and unlike painting with paints?

Variation: Crayon Wax Resist

Have students draw their designs on the fabric with crayons instead of using hot wax. Follow the same process as above. Note: The color from the crayons will remain after the wax has been absorbed by the paper.

2—Silk Painting with Dyes

Science, Social Studies, Art

Preparation

Have a variety of silk scarves or other pieces of silk that have been dyed available for the students to examine. Encourage the students to feel the textures and to talk about the designs. Explain that in many parts of the world, people decorate silk by dying it.

With the students, or ahead of time, wash the silk with warm water and a mild detergent. Hang to dry. While it is still damp, iron to remove wrinkles. Demonstrate how to draw with the resist and paint on the dye to color the fabric (using resist is optional). Rock salt can be used to make interesting designs. Sprinkle salt on the fabric immediately after it has been painted (while still wet) and leave it until the fabric is dry. Ask students to describe what happens, and why. Follow the directions on the bottle of dye to set the fabric.

∅ ∅ ∅

In the activity that follows, involve the students in painting silk designs of their own.

Each Student Needs

- Silk dyes (available at many hobby stores and some discount stores, and in kits)
  Be sure to follow directions on the dye bottles.
- Silk dye set
- Silk dye resist
- Paintbrushes
- Optional: Rock salt
- White silk blanks (available where silk dye is sold)
- Water
- Large piece of cardboard
- Iron
    Safety Note: The iron is very hot. Don't let it touch any part of your body.

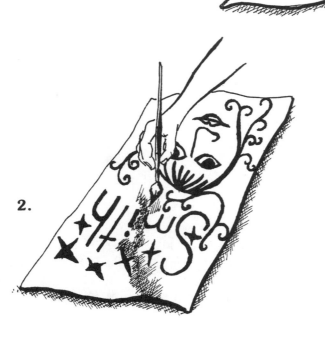

1.

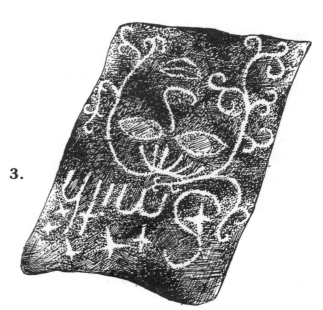

2.

3.

Steps for Coloring Silk

Have Each Student

1. Decide what designs you want to put on the silk. Squirt the resist to make the designs (resist will outline the individual shapes so they will not bleed together).
2. Paint the dye on the fabric.
3. Optional: Sprinkle salt on the wet dye to create unusual designs.
4. Let the fabric dry. Set the dyes by dipping the fabric in silk dye set.
5. Iron the fabric when it is completely dry.

Exploring with Students

Are you creating a picture or a design? What did you learn as you worked with the resist and dyes?

Variation

For a variation on the activity above, have students try a combined sun technique. Use transparent dyes, dilute with water (one part dye to two parts water). Stretch the fabric in an embroidery hoop (a small or large hoop works well). Paint the fabric with the dyes and, while the fabric is wet, apply a paper cutout, a natural material such as a leaf, or another small item such as a beaded necklace or key. (Sunlight reacts with the dye, so the fabric beneath these objects will be lighter in color than the rest of the fabric.) Place the fabric (still in the hoop) in the sunlight until it is completely dry. Remove the objects. This technique also works well with white, cotton fabric, and the dye can be set by ironing.

Fabric Dried in Sun

3—Tie-Dyeing Cloth

Art, Social Studies, Science

Preparation

Dyeing cloth is still a popular method of decorating fabric. Have students help push a light-colored piece of tied fabric into a bucket or tub containing water and clothing dye (using a wood spoon or a stick). Help them remove the fabric, wash it under cool water, wring out the water, and hang it to dry. Involve them in describing the process of tie-dyeing cloth.

After the students have discussed and experimented with the concept of tie-dyeing cloth, explain that people in India have decorated cloth since the beginning of recorded history. Tie-dyeing, which has been popular in India, dates back to 700 B.C.E. The original dyes were made from berries, bark, roots, fruit, flowers, and other natural materials.

✇ ✇ ✇

In the activity that follows, involve students in experimenting with the varied and exciting technique called tie-dyeing.

Each Student (or Group) Needs

- Clothing dye of various colors (prepared following directions on package)
- Buckets or coffee cans
- Wooden spoons or sticks
- Pieces of white fabric
- Rubber bands
- Paint shirts to protect students' clothing from the dye

Have Each Student (or Group)

1. Mix the dyes, using a wooden spoon or stick.
2. Experiment with tying and knotting the fabric before it is dipped into the dye. These are three common ways to tie the fabric to create dye patterns:

    Bull's-eye Knot (see p. 161)

    Small Knobs (see p. 162)

    Twisting Rope (see p. 163)
3. Have students dye a piece of fabric using a more controlled method to make a design or scene. For example, have available a bucket of each of several colors of dye. Have students proceed from bucket to bucket, carefully dipping sections of the fabric into the various dyes.
4. Rinse the fabric with cold water.
5. Undo the knots and hang the fabric to dry.
6. Repeat the process if additional colors and patterns are desired.

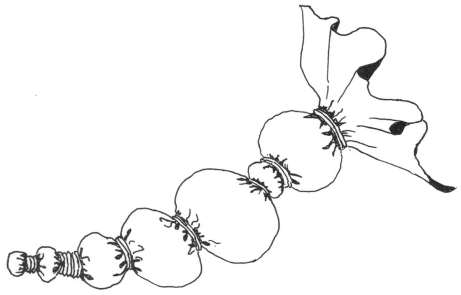

Bull's-eye Knot

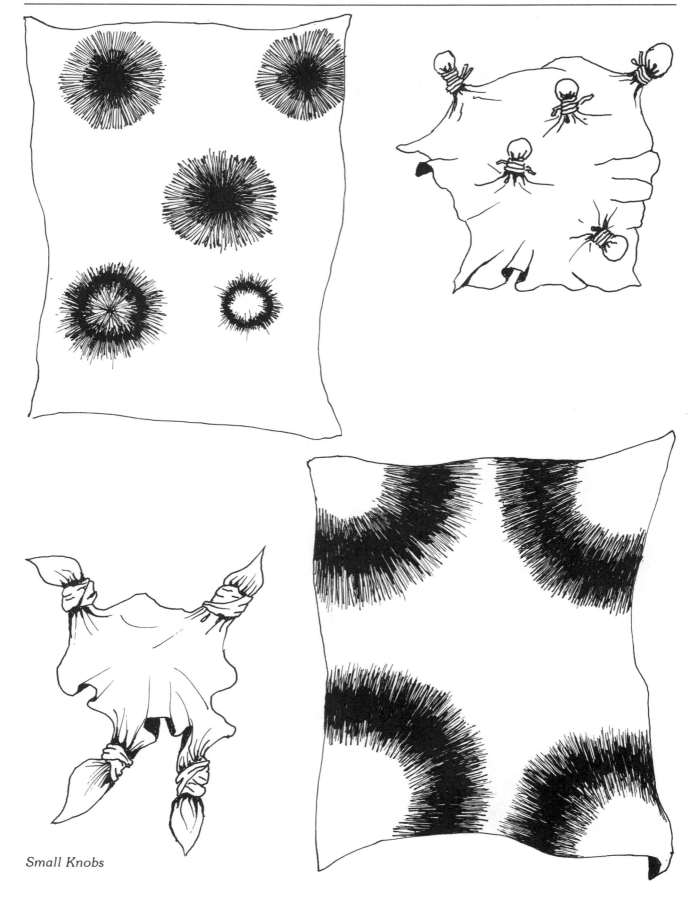

Small Knobs

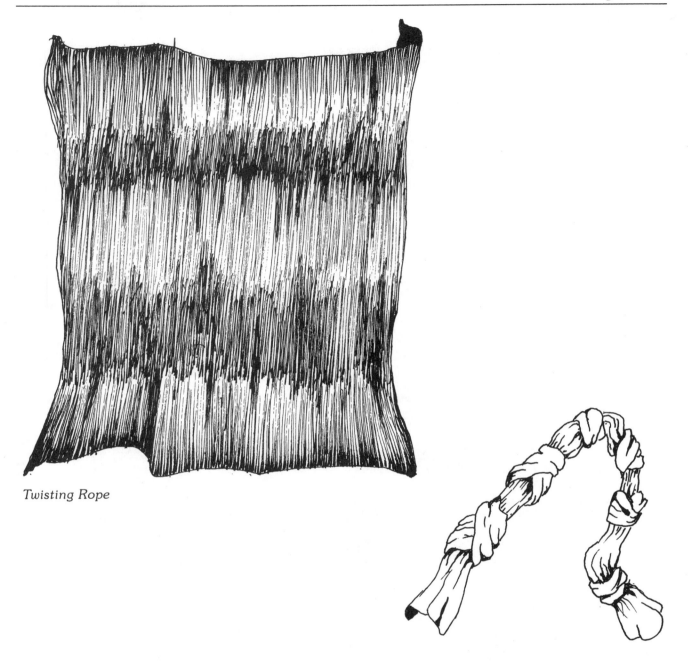

Twisting Rope

Exploring with Students

What kind of design do you think your knots and dyes will make? If you are dying one color over another, what third color will be created? Can you think of a fourth tying method?

Variation

T-shirts work exceptionally well for tie-dyeing. Some students have tie-dyeing birthday parties. Each student experiments with coloring their shirt in a personal way, and then wears the result proudly!

Weaving

For many years, people have been weaving cloth—on standing looms and on back-strap looms pulled across their waists. Have various weavings available for students to examine. Perhaps there are people in your community who have weavings from other parts of the world. Let the students feel the different textures, and discuss the fineness and colors of the weaves. Involve students in thinking about the process of weaving cloth, and about the people who do it.

1—Maximina

Social Studies, Art

Preparation

Read to students the account of Maximina, a Mayan weaver, as a prelude to the activities that follow.

Maximina with Her Loom

Maximina the Weaver

Maximina lives in San Antonio Aguas Calientes, a small village in Central America. She is Mayan, and speaks Cakchiquel and Spanish. Her house is at the base of a volcano. Maximina learned to weave from her mother when she was seven years old, and she has taught her students to weave. Her weavings are brightly colored and beautiful.

Maximina weaves on a back-strap loom. This is a loom that goes around a person's waist. It takes a lot of skill and care to weave the fine threads into cloth. The designs Maximina weaves are in her head, taught to her by her mother. The weaving takes a lot of time, but she likes being an artist. She knows that her work is beautiful, and that many people enjoy her weavings.

If the threads are light in color, Maximina can weave at night in the moonlight, but if the threads are darker, she weaves during the day at her shop. Her shop is in Antigua, Guatemala, and Maximina goes there every morning on the bus. Sometimes her daughters go with her. They also weave colorful wall hangings. During the day, they laugh and talk with one another and the tourists and friends who come to the shop. At the end of each long day, they get back on the bus and ride home to their house at the base of the volcano.

Activities

1. Discuss the story about Maximina. The students may be interested in knowing that her village is built on the Agua Volcano. *Agua* is the Spanish word for "water." The volcano is still active but has not erupted for some time.

2. The weaving thread used by the Mayan people was originally made from goat or sheep wool. It was dyed with natural materials in the area. Now they buy their thread, but it is not as strong. Pass around a piece of material that has been woven with thread. Encourage the students to examine the fineness of the weaving. Pass around a rug or wall hanging that has been woven with yarn. How is it different? Would it take more or less time to weave with yarn rather than thread? What would the advantages be for each type of weaving (such as weight and warmth of garment, and use of weaving)?

3. Read to students the book *Abuela's Weave* (1993) by Omar S. Castañeda, a story about a girl and her grandmother who weave on back-strap looms in Central America. Discuss the story with the students and examine the illustrations.

4. For an additional glimpse of Mayan life, read to students the book *The Most Beautiful Place in the World* (1988) by Ann Cameron.

2—Standing Looms

Art, Science, Music

Preparation

Create a standing loom for the class. Wood floor looms can be made simply and provide hours of intriguing activity as students experiment with weaving brightly colored yarn and other materials. Create a simple loom following the pattern below, and then encourage students to bring to class various materials to incorporate into the weaving. Loom kits are also available for purchase.

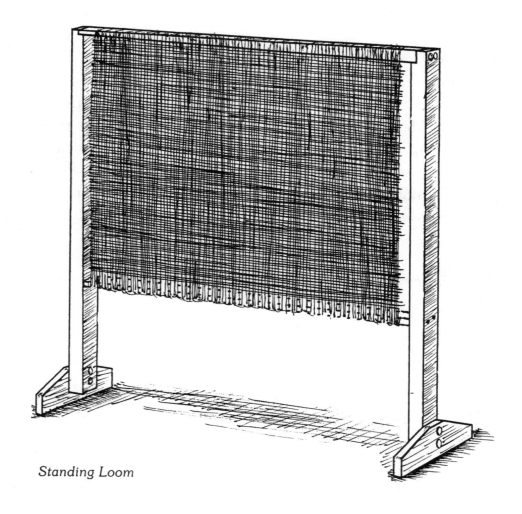

Standing Loom

Materials for Loom

- Weaving comb
- Yarn for weaving—several skeins of various colors
- Optional: Feathers, fabric strips, bark, and straw can also be used for weaving

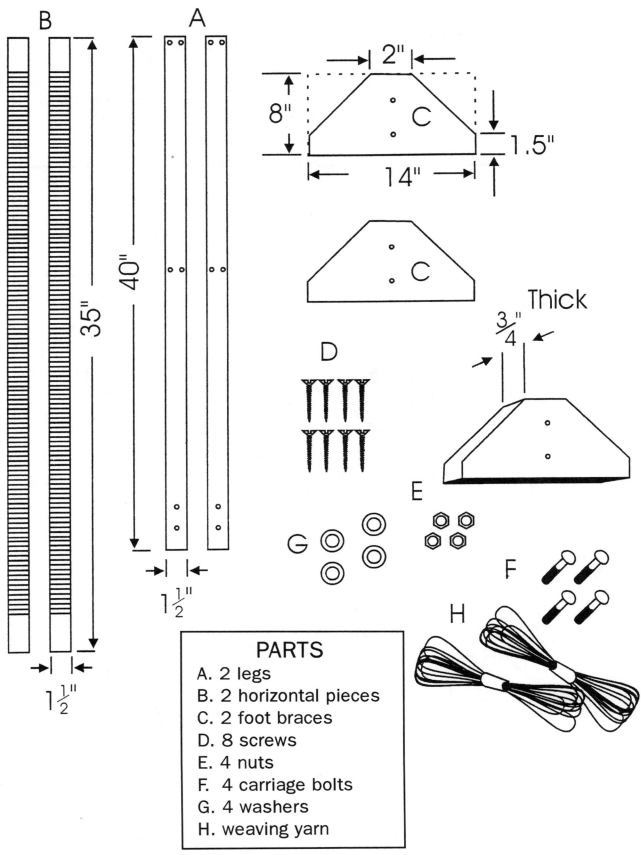

B

A

2"

8"

C

1.5"

14"

35"

40"

C

Thick

$\frac{3}{4}$"

D

E

G

1$\frac{1}{2}$"

1$\frac{1}{2}$"

F

H

PARTS
A. 2 legs
B. 2 horizontal pieces
C. 2 foot braces
D. 8 screws
E. 4 nuts
F. 4 carriage bolts
G. 4 washers
H. weaving yarn

Materials for Loom

Construction of Loom

1. Cut the wood and drill holes.
2. Attach legs to horizontal pieces.
3. Attach the foot braces to legs.
4. File impressions $\frac{1}{16}$ inch deep and $\frac{1}{4}$ inch apart on top and bottom of horizontal pieces. (Use a file or a hacksaw.)
5. Thread the loom with yarn. (Use library sources for information.)

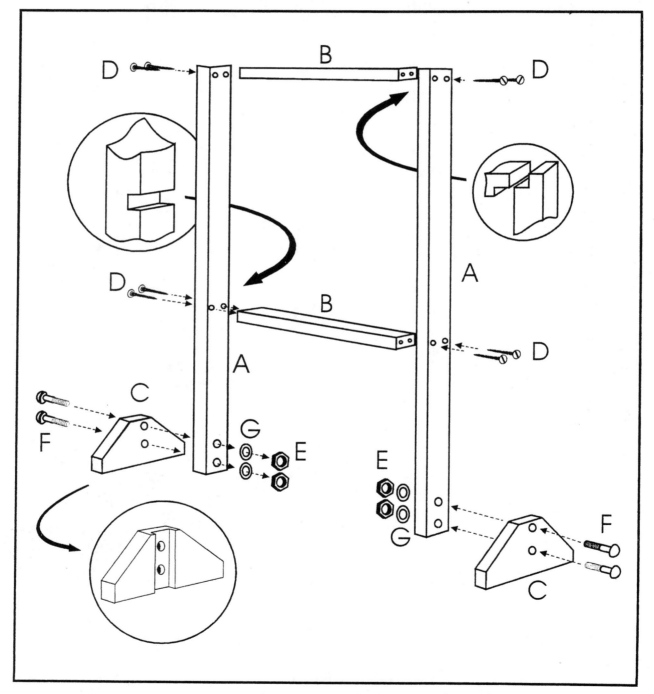

Construction of Loom

Have Each Student (or Group)

1. Weave yarn across the warp on the loom. After each row is woven, pack the yarn with a weaving comb.
2. When the weaving is complete, cut it away from the loom by cutting all the yarn at the top and bottom of the weaving. Tie off each pair of yarn ends.

Exploring with Students

What other materials could be incorporated into the weaving? String, leaves, feathers, dried flowers, cotton, straw?

Extending Ideas

1. Many students will not be familiar with weaving a Maypole and will enjoy participating in a May Day celebration. Have students sing the song " 'Round the Maypole" (see p. 170), in a round, as they weave the ribbons around the pole. A Maypole is a pole that is decorated with ribbons. The ribbons hang from the top of the pole. People dance around the pole on May Day. Each person holds the end of a ribbon. As they dance around the pole, participants weave around each other to create a woven design of ribbons wrapped around the pole.

Maypole

'ROUND THE MAYPOLE

O- ver, un- der, in and out; Danc- ing high and low.

'Round the may- pole fol- low me; Wea- ving as we go.

Bibliography

Armstrong, William H. *Barefoot in the Grass: The Story of Grandma Moses*. Garden City, NY: Doubleday, 1970.

Blood, Charles L., and Martin A. Link. *The Goat in the Rug*. New York: Aladdin Books; Macmillan, 1990.

Brand, Oscar. *When I First Came to This Land*. 1957. Reprint, New York: Ludlow Music, 1965.

Bunting, Eve. *Night Tree*. San Diego, CA: Harcourt Brace Jovanovich, 1991.

Cameron, Ann. *The Most Beautiful Place in the World*. New York: Bullseye Book/Random House, 1988.

Carrick, Carol. *Whaling Days*. New York: Houghton Mifflin, 1993.

Castañeda, Omar S. *Abuela's Weave*. New York: Lee & Low Books, 1993.

Clark, Ann Nolan. *Little Herder in Autumn*. Santa Fe, NM: Ancient City Press, 1988.

Cohen, Caron Lee. *The Mud Pony*. New York: Scholastic, 1988.

dePaola, Tomie. *The Legend of the Bluebonnet*. New York: Putnam, 1983.

———. *The Legend of the Indian Paintbrush*. Hong Kong: South China Printing, 1988.

———. *The Quilt Story*. New York: Putnam, 1985.

Dorros, Arthur. *Tonight Is Carnaval*. New York: Dutton Children's Books, 1991.

Ferguson, Dale, and James Giblin. *The Scarecrow Book*. New York: Crown, 1980.

Flournoy, Valerie. *The Patchwork Quilt*. New York: Dial Books for Young Readers/Division of E. P. Dutton, 1985.

Franklin, Kristine L. *The Shepherd Boy*. New York: Macmillan, 1994.

Garaway, Margaret Kahn. *The Old Hogan*. Cortez, CO: Ute Mountain, 1991.

Gershator, Phillis. *Tukama Tootles the Flute: A Tale from the Antilles*. New York: Orchard Books, 1994.

Glubok, Shirley. *The Art of Africa*. New York: Harper & Row, 1965.

Goble, Paul. *Love Flute*. New York: Bradbury Press/Macmillan, 1992.

Hadley, Eric, and Tessa Hadley. *Legends of the Sun and Moon*. New York: Press Syndicate of the University of Cambridge, 1983.

Hall, Donald. *The Ox Cart*. Illustrated by Barbara Cooney. New York: Viking Press, 1976.

Horwitz, Elinor. *Contemporary American Folk Artists*. Philadelphia: Lippincott, 1975.

Johnston, Tony, and Tomie dePaola. *The Quilt Story*. New York: Putnam, 1985.

Jones, Iris Sanderson. *Early North American Dollmaking: A Narrative History and Craft Instructions*. San Francisco: 101 Productions, 1976.

Kachina Dolls: Form and Function in Hopi Tithu. Plateau 54, no. 4. Flagstaff, AZ: Museum of Northern Arizona, 1990.

Kalman, Bobbie. *Homes Around the World*. New York: Crabtree, 1994.

Kelly, Karin. *Weaving*. Minneapolis, MN: Lerner, 1973.

Kesselman, Wendy. *Emma*. New York: Doubleday, 1980.

Knight, Margy Burns. *Talking Walls*. Gardiner, ME: Tilbury House, 1992.

Maher, Ramona. *Alice Yazzie's Year*. New York: Coward, McGann & Geohegan, 1977.

Martin, Patricia Miles. *Navajo Pet*. New York: G. P. Putnam's Sons, 1971.

McQuiston, Don, and Debra McQuiston. *Dolls & Toys of Native America: A Journey Through Childhood*. San Francisco: Chronicle Books, 1995.

Mendez, Phil. *The Black Snowman*. New York, Scholastic, 1989.

Miles, Miska. *Annie and the Old One*. Boston: Joy Street/Little, Brown, 1990.

Morris, Ann. *Houses & Homes*. New York: Lothrop, Lee & Shepard, 1992.

O'Kelley, Mattie Lou. *From the Hills of Georgia: An Autobiography in Paintings*. Boston: Atlantic Monthly Press/Little, Brown, 1983.

Oneal, Zibby. *Grandma Moses, Painter of Rural America*. Women of Our Time. New York: Viking Penguin, 1986.

Pinkwater, Daniel. *The Big Orange Spot*. New York: Scholastic, 1977.

Radlauer, Edward, and Ruth Shaw Radlauer. *What Is a Community?* Chicago; Los Angeles: Elk Grove Press, 1967.

Rae, Mary Maki. *The Farmer in the Dell*. New York: Viking/Kestral, 1978.

Ringgold, Faith. *Aunt Harriet's Underground Railroad in the Sky*. New York: Crown/Random House, 1992.

———. *Faith Ringgold: Tar Beach*. New York: Crown, 1991.

Robbins, Chandler S., Bertel Brunn, and Herbert S. Zim. *A Guide to Field Identification: Birds of North America.* New York: Golden Press, 1966.

Rosenak, Chuck, and Jan Rosenak. *The People Speak: Navajo Folk Art.* Flagstaff, AZ: Northland, 1994.

Safran, Sheri. *My Grandmother's Patchwork Quilt: A Book and Pocketful of Patchwork Pieces.* New York: Delacorte Press/Bantam Doubleday Dell, 1993/1994.

Smith, MaryLou M. *Grandmother's Adobe Dollhouse.* Santa Fe: New Mexico Magazine/Nuevo West Book, 1984.

————. *La abuelita y su casa de munecas.* New York: Scholastic, 1993.

Sohi, Morteza E. *Look What I Did with a Leaf!* New York: Walker, 1993.

Spier, Peter, illus. *The Fox Went Out on a Chilly Night: An Old Song.* Garden City, NY: Doubleday, 1961.

Stein, R. Conrad. *The Story of the New England Whalers.* Chicago: Childrens Press, 1982.

Stokes, William Michael, and William Lee Stokes. *Messages on Stone: Selections of Native Western Rock Art.* Salt Lake City, UT: Starstone, 1980.

Swentzell, Rina. *Children of Clay: A Family of Pueblo Potters.* Minneapolis, MN: Lerner, 1992.

Terzi, Marinella. *Prehistoric Rock Art. The World Heritage. Chicago: Childrens Press, 1992.*

Trimble, Stephen. *The Village of Blue Stone.* New York: Macmillan, 1990.

Turner, Robyn Montana. *Faith Ringgold.* Portraits of Women Artists for Children. Boston: Little, Brown, 1993.

Wilder, Laura Ingalls. *Little House in the Big Woods.* New York: Harper & Row, 1932.

Winter, Jeanette. *Diego.* New York: Borzoi Book/Alfred A. Knopf, 1991.

Zuromskis, Diane, illus. *The Farmer in the Dell.* Boston: Little, Brown, 1978.

Index

About the Author

Susan Thompson, Ed.D., began her career in education as a second grade teacher in the mining community of Hanna, Wyoming. She is currently an assistant professor of education and director of elementary education programs for the University of Wyoming Casper College Center. Susan has loved folk art since she was young and enjoys friendships with many artists in different parts of the world. Susan has shared many creative ideas through the books she has written, which include *Hooray for Clay!*, *Natural Materials*, and *Elephants Are Wrinkly*. She has also written a children's book, *James Joe: Autobiography of a Navajo Medicine Man*, published by the Council of Indian Education. Susan lives with two daughters, Kayenta and Rosalie, and with her husband Keith, who is a geologist. All of them appreciate, love, and create art.

From **Teacher Ideas Press**

ONE VOICE: Music and Stories in the Classroom
Barbara M. Britsch and Amy Dennison-Tansey

This treasury of improvisational music and drama, child-centered art, child-created story productions, and other outstanding activities emphasizes student participation and empowers young people to experience the imaginative possibilities of music and storytelling. **Grades K–6**.
xxiv, 175p. 8½x11 paper ISBN 1-56308-049-4

ARTSTARTS: Drama, Music, Movement, Puppetry, and Storytelling Activities
Martha Brady and Patsy T. Gleason

Selected as Editor's Choice by *Learning Magazine*, this book makes it easy to integrate the arts into the classroom. Teachers and students alike love its lively integrated approach and classroom-tested activities. **Grades K–6**.
xii, 219p. 8½x11 paper ISBN 1-56308-148-2

FIFTY FABULOUS FABLES: Beginning Readers Theatre
Suzanne I. Barchers

Involve young children in reading and learning with these charming readers theatre scripts based on traditional fables from around the world. Each has been evaluated with the Flesch-Kincaid Readability Scale and includes guidelines and tips for presentation, props, and delivery.
Grades 1–4.
x, 137p. 8½x11 paper ISBN 1-56308-553-4

MAGIC MINUTES: Quick Read-Alouds for Every Day
Pat Nelson

Guaranteed to spread a special magic over listeners and bring many minutes of enchantment to all, this collection of short stories celebrates tried-and-true wisdom from around the world, as well as old-time humor and new-time heroes. **All Levels**.
xv, 151p. paper ISBN 0-87287-996-8

DAY OF THE MOON SHADOW: Tales with Ancient Answers to Scientific Questions
Judy Gail and Linda A. Houlding

This versatile resource offers brief, understandable, and fascinating scientific explanations to a multitude of questions, then leads readers to another time and culture to examine them.
Grades 2–6.
xx, 287p. 8½x11 paper ISBN 1-56308-348-5

TADPOLE TALES: Readers Theatre for Young Children
Anthony D. Fredericks

These wild and wacky adaptations of Mother Goose rhymes and traditional fairy tales will fill your classroom with laughter and learning! Featuring more than 25 reproducible scripts, an assortment of unfinished plays and titles, and practical guidelines for using readers theatre in the classroom, this book is a perfect resource for primary educators. **Grades 1–4**.
xii, 139p. 8½x11 paper ISBN 1-56308-547-X

For a FREE catalog or to place an order, please contact:

Teacher Ideas Press
Dept. B57 · P.O. Box 6633 · Englewood, CO 80155-6633
1-800-237-6124, ext. 1 · Fax: 303-220-8843 · E-mail: lu-books@lu.com

 Check out the TIP Web site!
www.lu.com/tip